ÆSOP

CARRIGBOY CLASSICS SERIES

ÆSOP

❧·❧

The Life of Æsop
Fables from Æsop

❧·❧

TRANSLATED BY

Sir Roger L'Estrange, 1692

COMPILED AND EDITED BY

Simon Prichard

CARRIGBOY CLASSICS

Published by
CARRIGBOY
Wells, Somerset, England.
www.carrigboy.co.uk
typecarrigboy@btinternet.com

© CARRIGBOY 2014

Print edition ISBN 978-1-910388-08-2
ePub/eBook ISBN 978-1-910388-07-5

A CIP catalogue record for this book is available from the British Library.

Cover design and print origination by CARRIGBOY.
Printed by CreateSpace.

CONTENTS

THE LIFE OF ÆSOP

Æsop's Fables

FOREWORD

CARRIGBOY CLASSICS SERIES

Welcome to the CARRIGBOY CLASSICS SERIES, a specially chosen series of books drawn from the very best of the World's classical literature.

CARRIGBOY CLASSIC titles are simultaneously re-typeset and published in both traditional print and eBook formats, all from the same, original and unabridged source material.

CARRIGBOY have been designing and typesetting historical and academic works for over twenty years, and you can be assured of the highest professional standards, and a book designed to ensure that the presentation does not obscure the content; that the format is immediately apparent, consistent and clear; and that the reading of a CARRIGBOY CLASSIC is always a taken-for-granted pleasure.

At CARRIGBOY we welcome suggestions for classical works you would like to see in matching print and eBook formats. Please don't hesitate to email us at the address on the copyright page if you have a request. No matter how unusual, we'll do our best to fulfil it.

INTRODUCTION

THE LIFE AND FABLES OF ÆSOP

ÆSOP was probably a real person; although it is impossible to be sure which of the surviving stories were really his. The date given him by Herodotus is about 570 B.C., and there is nothing to make this date improbable. Other ancient sources include Aristotle and Plutarch, who has him dining with the Seven Sages of Greece and sitting beside his friend Solon, whom he had met in Sardis. The earliest known writings appear from the first century A.D. Later, stories of this kind, especially animal stories, were all ascribed to Æsop, and the Greek collection which goes under his name contains stories of many ages. A number of Æsop's fables are found in India, and it is not certain where they were first told.

Sir Roger L'Estrange, the translator of the present book, was born in 1616 and died in 1704. He was a staunch Royalist, an author and pamphleteer, and Member of Parliament for Winchester from 1685 to 1689.

He fought on the Royalist side in the English Civil War and was sentenced to death as a spy, spending four years in Newgate gaol, from which he escaped. During the Commonwealth he lived abroad, in Holland, returning to England at the Restoration to become Licenser of the Press (1663), in which role he was charged with the prevention of sedition and authorised to search the premises of printers and booksellers on the merest suspicion of dissension. L'Estrange excelled at his office. Hunting down and suppressing hidden presses and seizing seditious books or pamphlets, he become known as the "Bloodhound of the Press."

He published a great many books himself, besides pamphlets and other ephemeral works. He translated *Josephus, Cicero on Friendship, Quevedo's Visions,* Senneca the Younger's *Morals,* and other works.

His Æsop, which includes fables drawn from other sources, was published in 1692, and has been often re-published through the years, his easy and vigorous colloquial style being well-suited to the subject.

THE LIFE

of

ÆSOP

❖ ❖ ❖

CHAPTER I

Of Æsop's Country, Condition, and Person

ÆSOP WAS BY birth of Greater Phrygia (though some will have him to be a Thracian, others a Samian), of a mean condition, and in his person deformed, to the highest degree: flat-nosed, hunch-backed, blobber-lipped; a long misshapen head; his body crooked all over, big-bellied, baker-legged, and his complexion so swarthy, that he took his very name from't; for Æsop is the same with Æthiop. And he was not only unhappy in the most scandalous figure of a man, that ever was ever heard of; but he was in a manner tongue-tied too, by such an impediment in his speech, that people could very hardly understand what he said. This imperfection is said to have been the most sensible part of his misfortune; for the excellency of his mind might otherwise have atoned in some measure, for the uncouth appearance of his person (at least if that part of his history may pass for current). There goes a tradition, that he had the good hap to relieve certain priests that were hungry, and out of their way, and to set them right again, and that for that good office he was, upon their prayers, brought to the use of his tongue. As to his impediment in his speech, whether there were any such thing or not, or how he came to be cured of it, the reader is at liberty what to believe and what not. And so likewise for twenty other passages up and down this history; some of them too trivial, and others too gross, to be taken notice of, upon this argument and occasion: let it suffice, that (according to the common tradition) he had been already twice bought and sold; and so we shall date the story of his adventures from his entrance into the service of at least a third master.

As to the age he lived in, it is agreed upon among the ancients, that it was when Crœsus governed Lydia; as also that Xanthus, a Samian, was his master.

CHAPTER II

Æsop and his Fellow-slaves upon their Journey to Ephesus

IT WAS ÆSOP's fortune to be sent to Ephesus, in company with other slaves to be sold. His master had a great many burdens to carry, and Æsop begged of his companions not to overcharge him. They found him a weakling, and bade him please himself. The parcel that he pitched upon was a pannier of bread; and twice as heavy as any of the rest. They called him a thousand fools for his pains, and so took up their luggage, and away they trudged together. About noon they had their dinner delivered out of Æsop's basket, which made his burden lighter by one half in the afternoon than it had been in the morning: and after the next meal he had nothing left him to carry but an empty basket. His fellow-slaves began now to understand, that Æsop was not so arrant a fool as they took him for; and that they themselves had not half the wit they thought they had.

CHAPTER III

Æsop is accused by False Witnesses for stealing his Master's Figs; and brings Himself off by his Wits, to the confusion of his Accusers

ÆSOP WAS NOT of a make to do his master much credit in the quality of a household-servant: so that he rather sent him abroad into the fields a digging, and to take care of his husbandry. By the time he had been there a while, his master went out after him to see how he went on with his work; and found everything done much to his satisfaction. In this interim comes a countryman to him with a present of most delicious figs; which he was so wonderfully delighted with, that he gave them in charge to his boy Agathopus to see them carefully laid up till he came back again from the bath, whither he was then a going. Æsop, it seems, was now gone home upon some particular business, and Agathopus laid hold of this occasion to tell one of his companions of a design he had, both upon the figs, and upon their fellow-servant. What have we more to do, says he, than to stuff our guts with these figs ourselves, and then lay the roguery upon Æsop, who is at this instant in the house where they are? And then, when our master comes to examine the matter, we are two witnesses to one against him, which will make it so clear a case, that the silly cur will not have the face to deny the fact. The plot, in short, was agreed upon; and to work they went upon the figs, making themselves merry upon every bit they swallowed, to consider how Æsop's carcass was to pay for all.

The master, upon his coming from the bath, called immediately for his figs, and hearing that Æsop had been beforehand with him, he sent for him in a rage, rattled him with a thousand traitors and villains for robbing his house, and devouring the fruit that he set apart for his own palate. This miserable wretch heard and understood all that was said; but by reason of an imperfection in his speech, he was not able to speak one word in his own defence. His enemies in mean time insulting over him, and calling for justice upon so insolent a cheat. They were now advancing from reproaches to blows, when Æsop cast himself at master's feet, and begged his patience only till he might go out and come in again. He went his way immediately, and fetched a vessel of warm water; took large draught of it in his master's presence, and with his finger in his throat brought it all clear up again without any other mixture. After this experiment upon himself he gave his master to understand, that if he would pleased to put his accusers to the same test, he should quickly see what was become of his figs. The proposal seemed so reasonable, that he ordered Agathopus and his fellow to do the like. They made some difficulty at first of following Æsop's example; but in the end, upon taking a soup of the same liquor, their stomachs wambled[1], up came the water, figs and all. Upon this evidence of the treachery and falsehood of Agathopus and companion, the master ordered them to be soundly lashed, and made good the old saying, harm watch, harm catch.

---

1 Weaved and rolled nauseously.

CHAPTER IV

The Sale of Æsop to Xanthus

UPON THE MERCHANT's arrival at Ephesus, he made a quick riddance of all his slaves but three. That is to say, a musician, an orator, and Æsop. He dressed up the two former in habits answerable to their profession, and carried them to Samos, as the likeliest place for a chapman². He shewed them there in the open market, with Æsop for a fool betwixt them; which some people took much offence at. While they were attending upon the place, there came, among other Samians, one Xanthus an eminent philosopher of that city, with a train of his disciples at his heels. The philosopher was mightily pleased with the two youths, and asked them one after another about their profession, and what they could do. The one told him he could do anything, the other that he could do everything; and this set Æsop laughing at 'em. The philosopher's pupils would needs know what it was that made Æsop so

---

2 A merchant, trader or peddler.

merry. Why, says he, if the question had been put by your master, I should have told him the reason of it.

Xanthus in the meantime was beating the price of the two other slaves, but the terms were so high, that he was just upon turning about to go his way, only the pupils would needs have him put the same questions first to the ill-favoured fellow that he had done to the other two; and so Xanthus, for the humour sake, interrogated Æsop what he could do. Nothing at all, says he. How comes that? says the philosopher. My companions, says the other, undertake everything, and there's nothing left for me to do. This gave them to understand, that the man knew well enough what he said, and what he laughed at. Well! says Xanthus, but if I should give money for you now, would you be good and honest? I'll be that, says Æsop, whether you buy me or no. Ay, but tell me again, says the philosopher, won't you run away? Pray, says Æsop, did you ever hear of a bird in a cage that told his master he intended to make his escape? Xanthus was well enough pleased with the turn and quickness of his wit; but, says he, that unlucky shape of yours will set people a hooting and gaping at you wherever you go. A philosopher, says Æsop, should value a man for his mind, not for his body. This presence of thought gave Xanthus a high opinion of the wisdom of the man; and so he bade the merchant set him his lowest price of that miserable creature. Why, says he, you had as good cheapen a dunghill; but if you'll bid me like a chapman for either of the other two, you shall have this phantom into the bargain. Very good, says the philosopher; and without any more ado what's your selling price? The merchant speaks the word, the philosopher pays the money, and takes Æsop away with him.

CHAPTER V

Xanthus presents Æsop to his Wife

XANTHUS HAD NO sooner made his purchase, and carried his jewel home with him, but, having a kind of a nice froward piece to his wife, the great difficulty was how to put her in humour for the entertainment of this monster, without throwing the house out at the window. My dear, says he, you have been often complaining of careless servants; and I have bought you one now that I am confident will fit your turn. He shall go and come and wait and do everything as you would have him. Oh, your servant, sweet heart, says she, but what did he cost you? Why truly very reasonable; but at present he's a little tanned and out of case, you must know, with his journey, says the husband, and so he ordered him to be called in. The cunning gipsy smoked[3] the matter presently. Some monster, says she, I'll be hanged else. Wife, wife, says Xanthus, if you are a good woman, that that pleases me must please you too. While these words

---

3 Understood.

were between his lips, up comes Æsop towards them; she gave him a fierce look, and immediately discharged her choler upon her husband. Is this a man, or a beast? says she, and what clearer proof in the world could you have given me now of an insufferable hatred and contempt? Æsop said not one word all this while, 'till Xanthus roused him with a reproof. Oh villain! says he; to have a tongue and wit at will upon all other occasions, and not one diverting syllable now at a pinch to pacify your mistress! Æsop, after a short pause upon't, bolted out an old Greek saying, which is in English to this effect, From lying at the mercy of fire, water, and a wicked woman, good Lord deliver us. If the wife was heartily angry before, this scum made her stark mad, and the reproach was so cutting too, that Xanthus bought himself off again from the malice of any ill intention, by a passage out of Euripides to this purpose: The raging of a tempestuous sea; the fury of a devouring fire; and the pinching want of necessaries for life, are three dreadful things, and a body might reckon up a thousand more; but all this is nothing to the terrible violences of an impetuous woman, and therefore, says he, make yourself as glorious on the other side, in the rank of good women. Upon this oblique admonition, the woman came to herself again, and took Æsop into her good graces, who rendered his master and mistress all the offices of a faithful servant.

CHAPTER VI

Æsop's Answer to a Gardener

SOME TWO OR three days after the encounter above mentioned, Xanthus took Æsop along with him to a garden to buy some herbs, and the gardener seeing him in the habit of a philosopher, told him the admiration he was in, to find how much faster those plants shot up that grow of their own accord than those that he set himself, though he took never so much care about them. Now you that are a philosopher, pray will you tell me the meaning of this? Xanthus had no better answer at hand than to tell him, that Providence would have it so; whereupon Æsop brake out into a loud laughter. Why how now, ye slave you, says Xanthus, what do you laugh at? Æsop took him aside and told him, Sir, I laugh at your master, that taught you no better; for what signifies a general answer to a particular question? And 'tis no news neither that Providence orders all things; but if you'll turn him over to me, you shall see I'll give him another sort of resolve. Xanthus told the gardener, that it was below a philosopher to busy his head about such trifles; but, says he, if you have a curiosity to be better informed, you should do well to ask my slave here and see what he'll say to you. Upon this, the gardener put the question to Æsop, who gave him this answer. The earth is in the nature of a mother to what she brings forth of herself out of her own bowels; whereas she is only a kind of a step-dame in the production of plants that are cultivated and assisted by the help and industry of another: so that it's natural for her to withdraw her nourishment from the one towards the relief of the other. The gardener, upon this, was so well satisfied, that he would take no money for his herbs, and desired Æsop to make use of his garden for the future as if it were his own.

CHAPTER VII

*Æsop's Invention to bring his Mistress back again to
her Husband after she had left him*

THE WIFE OF Xanthus was well-born and wealthy,
but so proud and domineering withal, as if her
fortune and her extraction had entitled her to the
breeches. She was horribly bold, meddling, and
expensive (as that sort of women commonly are);
easily put off the hooks, and monstrous hard to
be pleased again; perpetually chattering at her
husband, and upon all occasions of controversy,
threatening him to be gone. It came to this at last,
that Xanthus's stock of patience being quite spent,
he took up a resolution of going another way to
work with her, and of trying a course of severity,
since there was nothing to be done with her by
kindness. But this experiment, instead of mending
the matter, made it worse; for upon harder usage,
the woman grew desperate, and went away from
him in earnest. She was as bad 'tis true as bad might
well be, and yet Xanthus had a kind of hankering

for her still: beside that there was matter of interest in the case; and a pestilent tongue she had, that the poor husband dreaded above all things under the sun; but the man was willing, however, to make the best of a bad game, and so his wits and his friends were set at work, in the fairest manner that might be, to get her home again. But there was no good to be done in't it seems; and Xanthus was so visibly out of humour upon't, that Æsop in pure pity bethought himself immediately how to comfort him. Come master (says he) pluck up a good heart; for I have a project in my noddle that shall bring my mistress to you back again, with as good a will as ever she went from you. What does me Æsop, but away immediately to the market among the butchers, poulterers, fishmongers, confectioners, &c., for the best of everything that was in season. Nay he takes private people in his way too, and chops into the very house of his mistress's relations, as by mistake. This way of proceeding set the whole town agog to know the meaning of all this bustle, and Æsop innocently told everybody that his master's wife was run away from him, and he had married another; his friends up and down were all invited to come and make merry with him, and this was to be the wedding feast. The news flew like lightning, and happy were they could carry the first tidings of it to the run-away lady (for everybody knew Æsop to be a servant in that family). It gathers in the rolling, as all other stories do in the telling. The wife, that was in her nature violent and unsteady, ordered her chariot to be made ready immediately, and away she posts back to her husband: falls upon him with outrages of looks and language; and after the easing of her mind a little, No, Xanthus, says she, do not you flatter yourself with the hopes of enjoying another woman while I am alive. Xanthus looked upon this as one of Æsop's masterpieces; and for that bout all was well again betwixt master and mistress.

CHAPTER VIII

An Entertainment of Neats' Tongues

SOME FEW DAYS after the ratification of this peace, Xanthus invited several philosophers of his acquaintance to supper with him; and charges Æsop to make the best provision he could think of for their entertainment. Æsop had a wit waggish enough, and this general commission furnished him with matter to work upon. So soon as ever the guests were set down at the table, Xanthus calls for supper, and expected no less than a very splendid treat. The first service was neats' tongues sliced, which the philosophers took occasion to discourse and quibble upon in a grave formal way, as the tongue (for the purpose) is the oracle of wisdom, and the like. Xanthus, upon this, calls for a second course, and after that for a third, and so for a fourth, which were all tongues, over and over again still, only several ways dressed: some boiled, others fried, and some again served up in soup, which put Xanthus into a furious passion. Thou villain, says he, is this according to my order, to have nothing but tongues upon tongues? Sir, says Æsop, without any hesitation, since it is my ill fortune to fall under this accusation, I do appeal to all these learned persons, whether I have done well, or ill, and paid that respect to your order which I ought to do.

Your order was, that I should make the best provision that I could think of for the entertainment of these excellent persons, and if the tongue be the key that leads us into all knowledge, what could be more proper and suitable than a feast of tongues for a philosophical banquet?

When Xanthus found the sense of the table to be on Æsop's side; Well my friends, says he; pray will you eat with me to-morrow, and I'll try if I can mend your cheer; and Mr. Major-domo, says he to Æsop, let it be the care of your gravity and wisdom to provide us a supper tomorrow, of the very worst things you can think of.

CHAPTER IX

A Second Treat of Tongues

XANTHUS'S GUESTS MET again the next day according to the appointment; and Æsop had provided them the very same services of tongues and tongues over and over, as they had the night before. Sirrah (says Xanthus to his servant) what's the meaning of this; that tongues should be the best of meats one day, and the worst the other? Why Sir, says he, there is not any wickedness under the sun that the tongue has not a part in. As murders, treasons, violence, injustice, frauds, and all manner of baseness; for counsels must be first agitated, the matter in question debated, resolved upon, and communicated by words, before the malice comes to be executed in fact. Tongue whither wilt thou! (says the old proverb) I go to build (says the tongue) and I go to pull down.

This petulant liberty of Æsop galled his master to the very soul of him, and one of the guests, to help forward his evil humour, cried out, This fellow is enough to make a body mad. Sir (says Æsop), you have very little business to do of your own I perceive, by the leisure you have to intermeddle in other people's matters; you would find some other employment else than to irritate a master against his servant.

CHAPTER X

Æsop brings his Master a Guest that had no sort of Curiosity in him

XANTHUS LAID HOLD of the present occasion, and was willing enough to be furnished with a staff to beat a dog. Well Sirrah, says he, since this learned gentleman is too curious, go your ways and find me out a man that has no curiosity at all, or I'll lace your coat for ye. Æsop, the next day, walked the whole town over on this errand; and at last found out a slovenly lazy fellow lolling at his ease, as if he had nothing to do or to take care for; and so up to him he went in a familiar way, and invited him to his master's to supper. The clown made no ceremony of promising, but fell presently to asking what kind of man his master was. And what, says he,—are we going just now? (for this poor Devil looked upon a meal's meat gratis as a blessing dropped into his mouth out of the skies). Come (says Æsop), we are going this very moment; and wonderfully glad he was to find by the booby's discourse, that he had met with a man so fit for his purpose. Away they went together, and so straight into the parlour, where the blockhead throws himself down, dirty and beastly as he was, upon a rich couch. After a very little while, in comes Xanthus to supper, and asks Æsop who that man was. Why, this is the man, says Æsop, that you sent me for; that is to say, a man that has no curiosity in him at all. Oh that's very well, says Xanthus, and then told his wife in her ear, that if she would but be a loving and obedient wife to him, and do as he bade her, he would now save her longing, for, says he, I have been a great while seeking for an occasion to pick a quarrel with Æsop, and I have found it at last. After this whisper, Xanthus takes a turn in the parlour, and calls aloud to his wife. Hark ye, sweetheart, says he, go fetch some water, and wash the feet of my guest here. Away she goes, brings a basin to the side of the couch, where the clown was laid at his length, and bade him put forth his feet for her to wash them. Xanthus little thought he would have done it. But the clown, after a little stumble within himself, that 'twas fitter for the maid to do't than the mistress: Well, says he, if it be the custom of the family, 'tis not for me to be against it; and so he stretched forth his feet to the washing.

So soon as ever the company had taken off the edge of their stomachs, Xanthus calls for a bumper[4],

4 A drinking vessel filled to the brim.

and puts it into the hands of the clown, making no doubt but he would have allowed his host the honour of being his taster. The fellow, without any scruple, whips up the drink, and gives Xanthus the pot again empty, who was now the second time disappointed upon the matter of curiosity, or no curiosity at all. He had a mind still to be upon poor Æsop's bones, and made another trial of the humour of his guest. There was a particular dish that the clown fed very heartily upon. Xanthus fell into a rage against the cook for the ill-dressing of it, and threatened to have him brought and lashed in the very parlour. The bumpkin took no notice of it at all, but without speaking one word on the cook's behalf; it was nothing to him, he thought, what other people did with their servants.

They were come now to their cakes and pies, and the clown guttled upon them without mercy. Xanthus resolves then upon another trial; calls for his pastrycook and tells him, Sirrah, says he, you spoil everything that goes through your hands. There's neither spice nor any other seasoning here. The cook told him, that if they were either over or underbaked, it was his fault; but for the spice and seasoning, it was his mistress's, for it was all put in that she delivered. Nay wife, says Xanthus, if it sticks there, by all that's sacred, I'll treat you no better than if you were a slave bought with my money. Wherefore strip immediately and prepare for a dogwhip. Xanthus thought with himself, that if anything in the world could move this barbarous brute, he would have put in a word at least to save a woman of honour from so scandalous an indignity; but, says this loggerhead to himself, there's an old saying: What have we to do to quench other people's fires? And I'll e'en keep myself clear of other people's matters; only he took Xanthus by the hand indeed, and told him if he would but stay a little, he'd go fetch his own wife too, and so they might take the lash by turns. In one word, Xanthus missed his aim at last; and though he was troubled at the miscarriage, he could not but laugh yet at the simplicity of the man, and confess, that Æsop was in the right in bringing a person to him that had no curiosity at all.

CHAPTER XI

Æsop's Answer to a Magistrate

IT HAPPENED SOME few days after the last passage above, that Xanthus, having some business at the Public Hall, sent Æsop to see if there were any great throng of men there; a magistrate meets him upon the way, and asks him whither he was going? Why truly, says Æsop, I am going I know not whither. The magistrate took it that he bantered him, and bade an officer take him into custody and carry him to prison. Well, says Æsop, to the magistrate, is it not true now, that I did not know whither I was going? Can you imagine that when I came out of the house this morning, I had any thoughts of going to prison? The magistrate was well enough pleased at the fancy, and discharged him upon it; and so he went forward to the hall, where among a world of people, he saw one man arrest another upon an action of debt. The debtor pleaded poverty; but if he would compound for half, it should go hard but he'd make a shift to pick it up, he said. Well with all my heart, says the creditor, lay down the money upon the nail, and the business is done; for a man had better content himself with half, than lose all, and I reckon that money as good as lost, that a man must go to law for. Æsop upon this went back and told his master, that he had been at the hall and saw but one man there; this was a riddle to Xanthus; insomuch that he went himself to learn the truth of the matter. When he came to the place, he found the court extremely thronged, and turning short upon Æsop, in great indignation, Sirrah, says he, are all these people come since you told me there was but one man here? 'Tis very true, says Æsop, there was a huge crowd, and yet but one man that I could see in that vast multitude.

CHAPTER XII

Xanthus undertakes to drink the Sea Dry

THERE HAPPENED NOT long after this to be a merry meeting of philosophers; and Xanthus one of the company. Xanthus had already gotten a cup too much; and Æsop finding they were like to set out his hand: Sir, says he, 'tis the humour of Bacchus, they say, first to make men cheerful, and when they are past that, to make 'em drunk, and in the conclusion, to make them mad. Xanthus took offence at Æsop; and told him, that was a lecture for children. The cups went round, and Xanthus by this time had taken his load, who was mightily given to talk in his drink; and whatever was uppermost, out it came, without either fear or wit. One of the company observing the weak side of the man, took the opportunity of pumping him with several questions. Xanthus (says he) I have read somewhere, that it is possible for a man to drink the sea dry; but I can hardly believe it. Why, says Xanthus, I'll venture my house and land upon't, that I do't myself. They agreed upon the wager, and presently off went their rings to seal the conditions. But early the next morning, Xanthus missing his ring, thought it might be slipped off his finger, and asked Æsop about it. Why truly, says Æsop, I can say nothing to the losing of your ring; but I can tell you that you lost your house and land last night; and so Æsop told him the story on't, which his master it seems had utterly forgotten. Xanthus began now to chew upon the matter, and it went to the heart of him to consider, that he could neither do the thing nor yet get quit of his bonds. In this trouble of thoughts he consults Æsop (whose advice before he had rejected) what was to be done in the case. I shall never forget, says Xanthus, how much I owe you for your faithful services; and so with fair words Æsop was prevailed upon to undertake the bringing of him off. 'Tis impossible to do the thing (says he), but if I can find a way to dissolve the obligation, and to gain you credit by it over and above, that's the point I suppose that will do your business. The time appointed, says Æsop, is now at hand, wherefore do you set a bold face upon it, and go to the sea-side with all your servants and your trinkets about you, and put on a countenance, that you are just now about to make good your undertaking. You'll have thousands of spectators there, and when they are got together, let the form of the agreement and the conditions be read, which runs to this effect. That you are to drink up the sea by such a certain time, or to forfeit your house and land, upon such or such a consideration. When this is done, call for a great glass, and let it be filled with sea-water, in the sight of the whole multitude; hold it up then in your hand, and say as follows: You have heard, good people, what I have undertaken to do, and upon what penalty if I do not go through with it. I confess the agreement, and the matter of fact as you have heard it; and I am now about to drink up the sea; not the rivers that run into't. And therefore let all the inlets be stopped, that there be nothing but pure sea left me to drink, and I am now ready to perform my part of the agreement, but for any drinking of the rivers, there is nothing of that in the contract. The people found it so clear a case, that they did not only agree to the reason and justice of Xanthus's cause, but hissed his adversary out of the field; who in the conclusion made a public acknowledgment, that Xanthus was the wiser and better man of the two; but desired the contract might be made void, and offered to submit himself further to such arbitrators as Xanthus himself should direct. Xanthus was so well pleased with the character his adversary had given him, of a wise man, that all was passed over and a final end made of the dispute.

CHAPTER XIII

Æsop baffles the Superstition of Augury

IN THE DAYS of Æsop, the world was mightily addicted to augury; that is to say, to the gathering of omens from the cry and flight of birds. Upon this account it was, that Xanthus one day sent Æsop into the yard, and bade him look well about him. If you see two crows (says he) you'll have good luck after it, but if you should chance to spy one crow single, 'tis a bad omen, and some ill will betide you. Æsop stepped out and came immediately back again, and told his master that he had seen two crows. Hereupon Xanthus went out himself, and finding but one (for the other was flown away) he fell outrageously upon Æsop for making sport with him, and ordered him to be soundly lashed for't; but just as they were stripping him for the execution, in comes one to invite Xanthus abroad to supper. Well master, says Æsop, and where's the credit of your augury now? When I, that saw two crows, am to be beaten like a dog, and you, that saw but one, are going to make merry with your friends? The reason and quickness of this reflexion pacified the master for the present, and saved the poor fellow a sound whipping.

CHAPTER XIV

Æsop finds Hidden Treasure

AS XANTHUS WAS walking once among certain monuments, with Æsop at his heels, and plodding upon several epitaphs, there was one inscription in Greek letters, that Xanthus WITH all the skill he had could not tell what to make of. Well, says Æsop, let me see a little if I can uncipher it. And so after laying things and things together a while, Master, says he, what will you give me, if I find you out a pot of hidden treasure now? One half of it, says Xanthus, and your liberty. So Æsop fell to digging, a matter of four yards from the stone that had the inscription; and there found a pot of gold which he took up and delivered to his master; and claimed his promise. Well, says Xanthus, I'll be as good as my word; but you must first shew me how you came to know there was treasure by the inscription; for I had rather be master of that secret than of the very gold itself. Æsop innocently opened the whole matter to him. Look you, Sir, says he, here are these letters. *a*; *β*; *δ*; *o*; *ε*; *θ*; *χ*; which are to be thus interpreted, *a* stands for ἀποβὰς; *β* for βήματα; *δ* for τέσσαπα; *o* for ὀρύζας; *ε* for εὑρήσεις; *θ* for θησαυρόν; *χ* for χρυσίου; in English, Dig four paces from this place, and you shall find gold. Now, says Xanthus, if you are so good at finding out gold, you and I must not part yet. Come Sir, says Æsop (perceiving that his master played fast and loose with him), to deal freely with you, this treasure belongs to King Dionysius. How do you know that? says Xanthus. Why, by the very inscription, says Æsop: for in that sense, *a* stands for ἀπόδος; *β* for βασιλεῖ; *δ* for Διονυσίῳ; *o* for ὄν; *ε* for εὑρες; *θ* for θησαυρὸν; *χ* for χρυσίου; in English, Give Dionysius the gold you have found. Xanthus began to be afraid when he heard it was the king's money, and charged Æsop to make no words on't, and he should have the one half. 'Tis well, says Æsop; but this is not so much your own bounty yet, as the intention of him that buried it; for the very same letters direct the dividing of it. As for example once again now, *a* stands for ἀνελόμενοι; *β* for βαδίςαντες; *δ* for διελεςθε; *o* for ὄν; *ε* for εὕρετε; *θ* for θησαυρὸν; *χ* for χρυσίου; in English, Divide the gold that you have found. Why then, says Xanthus, let us go home and share it. No sooner were they got home, but Æsop was presently laid by the heels, for fear of blabbing, crying out as loud as he could, This comes of trusting to the faith of a philosopher. The reproach nettled his master: but however he caused his shackles to be taken off upon't, and admonished Æsop to keep his tongue in a little better order for the future, if ever he hoped to have his liberty. For that, says Æsop, prophetically, I shall not need to beg it of you as a favour, for in a very few days I shall have my freedom, whether you will or no.

CHAPTER XV

Æsop expounds upon an Augury, and is Made Free

ÆSOP HAD THUS far borne all the indignities of a tedious slavery, with the constancy of a wise man, and without either vanity or abjection of mind. He was not ignorant, however, of his own value; neither did he neglect any honest way or occasion of advancing his name and his credit in the world; as in one particular instance among the Samians, on a strange thing that happened there upon a very solemn day. The ring, it seems, that had the town-seal upon't was laid somewhere in sight, where an eagle could come at it; she took it up in the air, and dropped it into the bosom of a slave. The Samians took this for a foreboding, that threatened some dismal calamity to the state, and in a general consternation they presently called a council of their wise men; and Xanthus in the first place, to give their opinions upon this mysterious accident. They were all at a loss what to think on't; only Xanthus desired some few days time for further consideration. Upon this, he betook himself to his study, and the more he beat his brains about it, the further he found himself from any hope of expounding the secret. This put him into a deep melancholy; which made Æsop very importune, and impatient, to know the cause of it; with assurances, that he would serve his master in the affair, whatever it was, to the uttermost of his power. Xanthus hereupon laid the whole matter before him, and told him in conclusion, that he was not only lost in his reputation, but in danger to be torn to pieces by the rabble. When Æsop found how the case stood, Never trouble your head any further, says he, do but follow my advice, and I'll bring you off as well now as ever I did before. When you appear tomorrow to give in your answer, I would have you speak to the people after this manner.

"I need not tell your wisdoms, that so many heads so many minds, and so many several men so many several conceptions of things; nay and further, that every several art, or profession, requires a distinct faculty or disposition, that is more or less peculiar to itself. It is the custom of the world for people, in all cases where they are either ignorant or doubtful, to repair to men that have the reputation of philosophers, for counsel and satisfaction. But this, under favour, is a great mistake; for it is with philosophers, as it is, I say, with other arts and professions that have their functions apart the one from the other. Wisdom, 'tis true, may be called properly enough the knowledge of things divine and human, but will you therefore expect that a philosopher should do the office of a shoemaker or a barber, because the trades are conversant about human things? No no gentlemen; a man may be a great philosopher without any skill at all in the handling of the awl, or the razor. But if the question were concerning the government of life and manners, the nature of things celestial or terrestrial; the duties that we owe to God or man; you could not do better than repair to philosophers for satisfaction. But for reading upon prodigies; or commenting upon the flight of birds, or the entrails of beasts, these are things quite beside the philosopher's business. If there be anything you doubt of that falls under the cognizance of philosophy, I am ready to serve you in't; but your present point being augury, I shall take leave to acquaint you that a servant I have at home, is as likely to make a right judgment that way as any man I know. I should not presume to name a servant; neither perchance would you think fit to make use of one, if the necessity of your present distress were not a very competent and reasonable excuse."

Here's your speech, says Æsop; and your credit saved whether they'll hear me or not. If they send for me, the honour will be yours, in case I deliver myself to their liking, and the disgrace will be mine then if I miscarry. His master was pleased beyond measure with the advice, but he did not as yet understand whither it tended.

Xanthus presented himself early the next morning before the council, where he dilated upon the matter according to his instructions, and so referred them to his servant for the clearing of the difficulty. The people with one voice cried out, Where is he? Why does not he appear? Why has not his master brought him along with him? In short, Æsop was immediately fetched into the court; and at the very first sight of him, they all burst out a laughing by consent. This fellow, says one, may have skill perhaps in divining, but he has nothing that's human about him. Another asked where he was born, and whether or no blocks had the faculty of speech in his country. Æsop, upon this, addressed himself to the council.

"You have here before ye (says Æsop), an ungracious figure of a man, which in truth is not a subject for your contempt, nor is it a reasonable ground for your despair, upon the matter in question. One wise man values another for his understanding, not for his beauty; beside that the deformity of my person is no incapacity at all as to your business. Did you never taste delicious drink out of an ill-looked vessel? or did you never drink wine that was vapid, or eager,[5] out of a vessel of

---

5   Sour (Fr. *aigre*).

gold? 'Tis sagacity and strength of reason that you have occasion for, not the force of robust limbs, nor the delicacies of colour and proportion. Wherefore I must beseech ye not to judge of my mind by my body, nor to condemn me unheard." Upon this, they all cried out to him, if he had anything to say for the common good, that he would speak it. "With your favour (says he), it is for that end I presume, that ye have called me hither, and it is with a great zeal for your service that I stand now before ye. But when I consider the weight of the matter in hand, and the office that I am now to perform, it will as little stand with your honours perhaps to take the opinion of a slave into your councils and debates, as it will with my condition to offer it; beside the risk I run of my master's displeasure upon the event. But all this may yet be obviated, my fears secured, my modesty gratified, and your own dignity preserved, only by making me a freeman beforehand, to qualify me for the function." They all said it was a most reasonable thing, and presently treated about the price of his liberty, and ordered the quæstors to pay down the money. When Xanthus saw that the thing must be done, he could not decently stand haggling about the price; but making a virtue of necessity, he chose rather to present Æsop to the commonwealth than to sell him. The Samians took it very kindly, and Æsop was presently made a citizen in form, proclaimed a freeman; and after this ceremony he discoursed upon the subject of the portent as follows.

"I shall not need to tell so many wise and knowing men, that the eagle is a royal bird and signifies a great king; that the dropping of the ring in the bosom of a slave that has no power over himself, portends the loss of your liberties, if you do not look to yourselves in time; and that some potent prince has a design upon ye." This put the Samians all a-fire to hear the issue of the prediction. In some short time after there came ambassadors from Crœsus the king of Lydia, to demand a tribute on the behalf of their master, and threatened the Samians with a war in the case of a refusal. This affair came to be debated in the council, where the majority was rather for peace with slavery, than for running the risk of a dispute; but they would not come to a resolution yet, without first consulting Æsop what they had best to do; who gave them his thought upon't in words to this effect.

"Every man in this world has two ways before him, that is to say, first, the way of liberty, that's narrow and rugged at the entrance, but plainer and smoother still the further you go. Secondly, the way of servitude or slavery, that seems to be easy at first, but you'll find it afterwards to be full of intolerable difficulties." The Samians, upon these words, declared themselves unanimously for liberty, and that since they were at present free, they would never make themselves slaves by their own consent; so the ambassadors departed, and there was a war denounced.

When Crœsus came to understand the resolution the Samians had taken, and how inclinable they were to a compliance, 'till Æsop, by the power only of a few words, diverted them from it, he resolved to send for and discourse with Æsop. So he made an offer to the Samians, upon their sending Æsop to him, to put a stop at present to the course of his arms. When Æsop came to hear of their proposition, he told them that he was not against their sending of him, provided only that he might tell them one story before he left them.

"In old time (says he), when some beasts talked better sense than many men do nowadays, there happened to be a fierce war betwixt the wolves and the sheep, and the sheep, by the help of the dogs, had rather the better on't. The wolves, upon this, offered the sheep a peace, on condition only that they might have their dogs for hostages. The silly, credulous sheep agreed to't, and as soon as ever they had parted with the dogs, the wolves brake in upon them, and destroyed them at pleasure."

The Samians quickly smelt out the moral of this fable, and cried out, one and all, that they would not part with Æsop: but this did not hinder Æsop, however, from putting himself aboard, and taking a passage for Lydia with the ambassadors.

CHAPTER XVI

Æsop presents Himself before the King of Lydia

IMMEDIATELY UPON ÆSOP's arrival in Lydia, he presented himself before the king, who looking upon him with contempt, hatred, and indignation: Is this a man says he, to hinder the king of Lydia from being master of Samos? Æsop then with a reverence after the Lydian fashion, delivered what he had to say.

"I am not here (says he), great king, in the quality of a man that's given up by his country, or under the compulsion of any force; but it is of my own accord that I am now come to lay myself at your majesty's feet, and with this only request, that you will vouchsafe me the honour of your royal ear, and patience but for a few words.

"There was a boy hunting of locusts, and he had the fortune to take a grasshopper. She found he was about to kill her, and pleaded after this manner for her life. Alas (says she) I never did anybody an injury, and never had it either in my will or in my power to do't. All my business is my song; and what will you be the better for my death? The youth's heart relented and he set the simple grasshopper at liberty.

"Your majesty has now that innocent creature before you: there's nothing that I can pretend to but my voice, which I have ever employed so far as in me lay to the service of mankind."

The king was so tenderly moved with the modesty and prudence of the man, that he did not only give him his life but bade him ask anything further that he had a mind to, and it should be granted him. Why then, says Æsop (with that veneration, gratitude and respect that the case required), I do most humbly implore your majesty's favour for my countrymen the Samians. The king granted him his request, and confirmed it under his seal; beside that the piety of making that petition his choice was a further recommendation of him to his royal kindness and esteem.

Æsop, soon after this, returned to Samos with the news of the peace, where he was welcomed with all the instances of joy and thankfulness imaginable; insomuch that they erected a statue for him, with an inscription upon it, in honour of his memory. From Samos he returned afterwards to Crœsus, for whose sake he composed several of those apologues[6] that pass in the world to this

---

6 Allegories or moral fables.

day under his name. His fancy lay extremely to travelling; but above all other places, he had the greatest mind to see Babylon: to which end he got letters of recommendation from Crœsus to the king there: who, according to Herodotus, was a friend, and an ally of Crœsus's, and his name, Labynetus. But his curiosity led him first to pass through Greece, for the sake of the seven wise men, whose reputation was at that time famous all over the world. He had the good hap in his travels to find them at Corinth, together with Anacharsis, and several of their followers and disciples, where they were all treated by Periander at a villa of his not far from the town. This encounter was to the common satisfaction of the whole company; the entertainment philosophical, and agreeable; and among other discourses they had some controversy upon the subject of Government; and which was the most excellent form: Æsop being still for monarchy, and the rest for a commonwealth. He travelled thence, a while after, into Asia, and so to Babylon, according to his first intention.

CHAPTER XVII

*Æsop adopts Ennus. Ennus's Ingratitude and Falseness,
and Æsop's Good Nature*

IT WAS THE fashion in those days for princes to
exercise trials of skill in the putting and resolving of
riddles and intricate questions; and he that was the
best at the clearing or untying of knotty difficulties
carried the prize. Æsop's faculty lay notably that
way, and rendered him so serviceable to the king,
that it brought him both reputation and reward.
It was his unhappiness to have no children for the
comfort and support of his old age; so that with
the king's consent, he adopted a young man, who
was well born and ingenious enough, but poor; his
name was Ennus. Æsop took as much care of his
institution[7] as if he had been his own child, and
trained him up in those principles of virtue and
knowledge that might most probably render him
great and happy. But there's no working upon a
flagitious and perverse nature, by kindness and

---

7 Education.

discipline, and 'tis time lost to think of mastering so insurable an evil: so that Ennus, after the manner of other wicked men, heaping one villainy upon another, counterfeits his father's name and hand to certain letters, wherein he promises his assistance to the neighbour princes against Labynetus. These letters Ennus carries to the king, and charges his father with treason, though in appearance, with all the trouble and unwillingness that was possible, only a sense of his duty to his king and his country swallowed up all other respects of reverence and modesty that a son owes to a father. The king took all these calumnies for instances of Ennus's affections to him, without the least suspicion of any fraud in the matter: so that without any further enquiry he ordered Æsop to be put to death. The persons to whom the care of his execution was committed, being well assured of his innocence and of the king's ungovernable passions, took him out of the way and gave it out that he was dead. Some few days after this, there came letters to Labynetus from Amasis the king of Egypt, wherein Labynetus was desired by Amasis to send him a certain architect that could raise a tower that should hang in the air, and likewise resolve all questions. Labynetus was at a great loss what answer to return, and the fierceness of his displeasure against Æsop being by this time somewhat abated, he began to enquire after him with great passion, and would often profess, that

if the parting with one half of his kingdom could
bring him to life again, he would give it. Hermippus
and others that had kept him out of the way told
the king upon the hearing of this, that Æsop was
yet alive; so they were commanded to bring him
forth; which they did, in all the beastliness he
had contracted in the prison. He did no sooner
appear, but he made his innocence so manifest, that
Labynetus in extreme displeasure and indignation
commanded the false accuser to be put to death
with most exquisite torments; but Æsop, after all
this, interceded for him and obtained his pardon,
upon a charitable presumption, that the sense of so
great a goodness and obligation would yet work
upon him.

CHAPTER XVIII

Æsop's Letters of Morality to his Son Ennus

UPON ÆSOP'S COMING again into favour, he had the king of Egypt's letter given him to consider of, and advised Labynetus to send him for answer, that early the next spring he should have the satisfaction he desired. Things being in this state, Æsop took Ennus home to him again, and so ordered the matter, that he wanted neither counsels nor instructions, nor any other helps or lights that might dispose him to the leading of a virtuous life, as will appear by the following precepts.

> "My son (says he), worship God with care and reverence, and with a sincerity of heart void of all hypocrisy or ostentation: not as if that divine name and power were only an invention, to fright women and children, but know that God is omnipresent, true, and almighty.

> Have a care even of your most private actions and thoughts, for God sees through you, and your conscience will bear witness against you.

It is according to prudence, as well as nature, to pay that honour to your parents that you expect your children should pay to you.

Do all the good you can to all men, but in the first place to your nearest relations, and do no hurt however where you can do no good.

Keep a guard upon your words as well as upon your actions, that there be no impurity in either.

Follow the dictates of your reason, and you are safe; and have a care of impotent[8] affections.

Apply yourself to learn more, so long as there's anything left that you do not know, and value good counsel before money.

Our minds must be cultivated as well as our plants; the improvement of our reason makes us like angels, whereas the neglect of it turns us into beasts.

There's no permanent and inviolable good, but wisdom and virtue, though the study of it signifies little without the practice.

Do not think it impossible to be a wise man, without looking sour upon it. Wisdom makes men severe, but not inhuman.

It is virtue not to be vicious.

Keep faith with all men. Have a care of a lie, as you would of sacrilege. Great babblers have no regard either to honesty or truth.

---

8 Overmastering.

Take delight in and frequent the company of good men, for it will give you a tincture of their manners too.

Take heed of that vulgar error, of thinking that there is any good in evil. It is a mistake when men talk of profitable knavery, or of starving honesty; for virtue and justice carry all that is good and profitable along with them.

Let every man mind his own business, for curiosity is restless.

Speak ill of nobody, and you are no more to hear calumnies than to report them: beside that, they that practice the one commonly love the other.

Propose honest things, follow wholesome counsels, and leave the event to God.

Let no man despair in adversity, nor presume in prosperity, for all things are changeable.

Rise early to your business, learn good things, and oblige good men; these are three things you shall never repent of.

Have a care of luxury and gluttony; but of drunkenness especially; for wine as well as age makes a man a child.

Watch for the opportunities of doing things, for there's nothing well done but what's done in season.

Love and honour kings, princes, and magistrates, for they are the bands of society, in punishing the guilty and protecting the innocent."

These, or such as these, were the lessons that Æsop read daily to his son; but so far was he from mending upon them, that he grew every day worse and worse, shewing that it is not in the power of art or discipline to rectify a perverse nature, or (as Euripides says) to make a man wise that has no soul. But however, he came soon after to be touched in conscience for his barbarous ingratitude, and died in a raging remorse for what he had done.

The spring was now at hand, and Æsop was preparing for the task he had undertaken about the building of a tower in the air, and resolving all manner of questions: but I shall say no more of that romantic part of the history, than that he went into Egypt, and acquitted himself of his commission to Amasis with great reputation. From thence back again to Labynetus, laden with honours and rewards; from whom he got leave to return into Greece; but upon condition of repassing to Babylon by the first opportunity.

CHAPTER XIX

Æsop's Voyage to Delphi; his Barbarous Usage there, and his Death

WHEN ÆSOP HAD almost taken the whole tour of Greece, he went to Delphi, either for the oracle's sake or for the sake of the wise men that frequented that place. But when he came thither, he found matters to be quite otherwise than he expected, and so far from deserving the reputation they had in the world for piety and wisdom, that he found them proud, and avaricious, and hereupon delivered his opinion of them under this fable.

"I find (says he) the curiosity that brought me hither, to be much the case of people at the seaside, that see something come hulling towards them a great way off at sea, and take it at first to be some mighty matter, but upon driving nearer and nearer the shore, it proves at last to be only a heap of weeds and rubbish."

The magistrates of the place took infinite offence at this liberty, and presently entered into a conspiracy against him to take away his life, for fear he should give them the same character elsewhere in his travels, that he had done there upon the place. It was not so safe they thought, nor so effectual a revenge to make him away in private; but if they could so contrive it, as to bring him to a shameful end, under a form of justice, it would better answer their business and design. To which purpose they caused a golden cup to be secretly conveyed into his baggage, when he was packing up to depart. He was no sooner out of the town upon his journey, but immediately pursued and taken upon the way by the officers, and charged with sacrilege. Æsop denied the matter, and laughed at them all for a company of mad men; but upon the searching of his boxes, they took the cup and shewed it to the people, hurrying him away to prison in the middle of his defence. They brought him the next day into the court, where notwithstanding the proof of his innocence, as clear as the day, he was condemned to die; and his sentence was to be thrown headlong from a rock, down a deep precipice. After his doom was past, he prevailed upon them, with much ado, to be heard a few words, and so told them the story of the Frog and the Mouse.

A Frog and a Mouse

There fell out a bloody quarrel once betwixt the Frogs and the Mice, about the sovereignty of the fens; and whilst two of their champions were disputing it at sword's point, down comes a kite powdering[9] upon them in the interim, and gobbles up both together, to part the fray.

This wrought nothing upon the hearts of the Delphians, but as they were bawling at the executioner to dispatch and do his office, Æsop on a sudden gave them the slip, and fled to an altar hard by there, in hopes that the religion of the place might have protected him, but the Delphians told him, that the altars of the Gods were not to be any sanctuary to those that robbed their temples; whereupon he took occasion to tell them the fable of the Eagle and the Beetle to this following effect.

An Eagle and a Beetle

A hare that was hard put to it by an Eagle, took sanctuary in a ditch with a Beetle. The Beetle interceded for the hare. The Eagle slapt off the former, and devoured the other. The Beetle took this for an affront to hospitality, as well as to herself, and so meditated a revenge, watched the Eagle up to her nest, followed her, and took her time when the Eagle was abroad, and so made a

---

9 "To come down with a powder" means with a rush or swoop.

shift to roll out the eggs, and destroy the brood. The Eagle upon this disappointment, timbered[10] a great deal higher next bout. The Beetle watched her still, and shewed her the same trick once again. Whereupon the Eagle made her appeal to Jupiter, who gave her leave to lay her next course of eggs in his own lap. But the Beetle found out a way to make Jupiter rise up from his throne; so that upon the loosening of his mantle, the eggs fell from him at unawares, and the Eagle was a third time defeated. Jupiter stomached the indignation, but upon hearing the cause, he found the Eagle to be the aggressor, and so acquitted the Beetle.

Now, says Æsop (after the telling of this fable), you are not to flatter yourselves that the profaners of holy altars, and the oppressors of the innocent, shall ever escape divine vengeance. This enraged the magistrates to such a degree, that they commanded the officers immediately to take Æsop from the altar, and dispatch him away to his execution. When Æsop found that neither the holiness of the place nor the clearness of his innocence was sufficient to protect him, and that he was to fall a sacrifice to subornation and power, he gave them yet one fable more as he was upon the way to execution.

"There was an old fellow (says he) that had spent his whole life in the country without ever seeing

---

10 Built.

the town; he found himself weak and decaying, and nothing would serve but his friends must needs shew him the town once before he died. Their asses were very well acquainted with the way, and so they caused them to be made ready, and turned the old man and the asses loose, without a guide, to try their fortune. They were overtaken upon the road by a terrible tempest, so that what with the darkness and the violence of the storm, the asses were beaten out of their way, and tumbled with the old man into a pit, where he had only time to deliver his last breath with this exclamation. Miserable wretch that I am, to be destroyed, since die I must, by the basest of beasts; by asses. And that's my fate now in suffering by the hands of a barbarous, sottish people, that understand nothing either of humanity or honour; and act contrary to the ties of hospitality and justice. But the Gods will not suffer my blood to lie unrevenged, and I doubt not but that in time the judgment of heaven will give you to understand your wickedness by your punishment."

He was speaking on, but they pushed him off headlong from the rock, and he was dashed to pieces with the fall.

The Delphians, soon after this, were visited with famine and pestilence, to such a degree that they went to consult the oracle of Apollo to know what wickedness it was that brought these calamities upon them. The oracle gave them this answer, that they were to expiate for the death of Æsop. In the conscience of their barbarity, they erected a pyramid to his honour, and it is upon tradition, that a great many of the most eminent men among the Greeks of that season went afterwards to Delphi, upon the news of the tragical end of Æsop, to learn the truth of the history, and found upon enquiry, that the principal of conspirators had laid violent hands upon themselves.

ÆSOP'S
FABLES

1

A Cock and a Diamond

AS A COCK was turning up a dunghill, he spied a Diamond. Well (says he to himself) this sparkling foolery now to a lapidary in my place would have been the making of him; but as to any use or purpose of mine, a barley-corn had been worth forty on't.

2

A Cat and a Cock

IT WAS THE hard fortune once of a Cock to fall into the clutches of a Cat. Puss had a month's mind to be upon the bones of him, but was not willing to pick a quarrel, however, without some plausible colour for't. Sirrah (says she) what do you keep such a bawling, and screaming a-nights for, that no body can sleep near you? Alas, says the Cock, I never wake any body, but when 'tis time for people to rise and go about their business. Come come, says Puss, without any more ado, 'tis time for me to go to breakfast, and cats don't live upon dialogues; at which word she gave him a pinch, and so made an end, both of the Cock, and of the story.

3

A Wolf and a Lamb

AS A WOLF was lapping at the head of a fountain, he spied a Lamb, paddling at the same time, a good way off down the stream. The Wolf had no sooner the prey in his eye, but away he runs open-mouth to't. Villain (says he) how dare you lie muddling the water that I'm a drinking? Indeed, says the poor Lamb, I did not think that my drinking there below, could have foul'd your water so far above. Nay, says t'other, you'll never leave your chopping of logic, till your skin's turned over your ears, as your father's was, a matter of six months ago, for prating at this saucy rate; you remember it full well, sirrah. If you'll believe me, sir (quoth the innocent Lamb, with fear and trembling), I was not come into the world then. Why thou impudence, cries the Wolf, hast thou neither shame, nor conscience? But it runs in the blood of your whole race, sirrah, to hate our family; and therefore since fortune has brought us together so conveniently, you shall e'en pay some of your forefathers' scores before you and I part; and so without any more ado, he leapt at the throat of the miserable helpless Lamb, and tore him immediately to pieces.

4

A Lion and a Bear

THERE WAS A Lion and Bear had gotten a fawn betwixt them, and there were they at it tooth and nail, which of the two should carry't off. They fought it out, till they were e'en glad to lie down, and take breath. In which instant, a fox passing that way, and finding how the case stood with the two combatants, seized upon the fawn for his own use, and so very fairly scampered away with him. The Lion and the Bear saw the whole action, but not being in condition to rise and hinder it, they passed this reflexion upon the whole matter; Here have we been worrying one another, who should have the booty, 'till this cursed fox has bobbed us both on't.

5

A Dog and a Shadow

AS A DOG was crossing a river, with a morsel of good flesh in his mouth, he saw (as he thought) another dog under the water, upon the very same adventure. He never considered that the one was only the image of the other; but out of a greediness to get both, he chops at the shadow and loses the substance.

6

A Lion, an Ass, etc., a Hunting

A LION, AN Ass, and some other of their fellow foresters, went a hunting one day; and everyone to go share and share alike in what they took. They plucked down a stag, and cut him up into so many parts; but as they were entering upon the dividend, Hands off says the Lion: this part is mine by the privilege of my quality; this, because I'll have it in spite of your teeth; this again, because I took most pains for't; and if you dispute the fourth, we must e'en pluck a crow about it. So the confederates' mouths were all stopped, and they went away as mute as fishes.

7

A Wolf and a Crane

A WOLF HAD got a bone in's throat, and could think of no better instrument to ease him of it, than the bill of a Crane; so he went and treated with a Crane to help him out with it, upon condition of a very considerable reward for his pains. The Crane did him the good office, and then claimed his promise. Why how now Impudence! (says t'other). Do you put your head into the mouth of a Wolf, and then, when y'ave brought it out again safe and sound, do you talk of a reward? Why sirrah, you have your head again, and is not that a sufficient recompense?

8

A Countryman and a Snake

A COUNTRYMAN HAPPENED in a hard winter to spy a Snake under a hedge, that was half frozen to death. The man was good natured and took it up, and kept it in his bosom, till warmth brought it to life again; and so soon as ever it was in condition to do mischief, it bit the very man that saved the life on't. Ah, thou ungrateful wretch! says he, is that venomous ill nature of thine to be satisfied with nothing less than the ruin of thy preserver?

9

A Lion and an Ass

AN ASS WAS so hardy once, as to fall a mopping and braying at a Lion. The Lion began at first to shew his teeth, and to stomack the affront; but upon second thoughts; Well! (says he) jeer on, and be an Ass still. Take notice only by the way, that 'tis the baseness of your character that has saved your carcass.

10

A City Mouse and a Country Mouse

THERE GOES AN old story of a Country Mouse that invited a City Sister of hers to a country collation, where she spared for nothing that the place afforded; as mouldy crusts, cheese-parings, musty oatmeal, rusty bacon, and the like. Now the City Dame was so well bred, as seemingly to take all in good part: But yet at last, Sister (says she, after the civilest fashion) why will you be miserable when you may be happy? Why will you lie pining, and pinching yourself in such a lonesome starving course of life as this is; when 'tis but going to town along with me, to enjoy all the pleasures, and plenty that your heart can wish? This was a temptation the Country Mouse was not able to resist; so that away they trudged together, and about midnight got to their journey's end. The City Mouse showed her friend the larder, the pantry, the kitchen, and other offices where she laid her stores; and after this, carried her into the parlour, where they found, yet upon the table, the reliques of a mighty entertainment of that very night. The City Mouse carved her companion of what she liked best, and so to't they fell upon a velvet couch together. The poor bumkin that had never seen, nor heard of such doings before, blessed herself at the change of her condition, when (as ill luck would have it) all on a sudden the doors flew open, and in comes a crew of roaring bullies, with their wenches, their dogs and their bottles, and put the poor mice to their wits' end how to save their skins. The stranger especially, that had never been at this sport before; but she made a shift however for the present, to slink into a corner, where she lay trembling and panting 'till the company went their way. So soon as ever the house was quiet again, Well, my Court Sister, says she, if this be the way of your town gambols, I'll e'en back to my cottage, and my mouldy cheese again; for I had much rather lie knabbing of crusts, without either fear or danger, in my own little hole, than be mistress of the whole world with perpetual cares and alarums.

11

A Crow and a Mussel

THERE WAS ONE of your Royston-Crows that lay battering upon a Mussel, and could not for his blood break the shell to come at the fish. A Carrion-Crow, in this interim, comes up and tells him, that what he could not do by force, he might do by stratagem. Take this Mussel up into the air, says the Crow, as high as you can carry it, and then let him fall upon that rock there; his own weight, you shall see, shall break him. The Roystoner took his advice, and it succeeded accordingly; but while the one was upon wing, the other stood lurching upon the ground, and flew away with the fish.

12

A Fox and a Raven

A CERTAIN FOX spied out a Raven upon a tree with a morsel in his mouth, that set his chops a watering; but how to come at it was the question. Oh thou blessed bird! (says he) the delight of Gods, and of men! and so he lays himself forth upon the gracefulness of the Raven's person, and the beauty of his plumes; his admirable gift of augury, &c. And now, says the Fox, if thou hadst but a voice answerable to the rest of thy excellent qualities, the sun in the firmament could not shew the world such another creature. This nauseous flattery sets the Raven immediately a gaping as wide as ever he could stretch, to give the Fox a taste of his pipe; but upon the opening of his mouth he drops his breakfast, which the Fox presently chopt up, and then bade him remember, that whatever he had said of his beauty, he had spoken nothing yet of his brains.

13

A Lion and a Mouse

UPON THE ROARING of a beast in the wood, a Mouse ran presently out to see what news: and what was it, but a Lion hampered in a net! This accident brought to her mind, how that she herself, but some few days before, had fallen under the paw of a certain generous Lion, that let her go again. Upon a strict enquiry into the matter, she found this to be that very Lion; and so set herself presently to work upon the couplings of the net; gnawed the threads to pieces, and in gratitude delivered her preserver.

14

A Swallow and Other Birds

THERE WAS A country fellow at work a sowing his grounds, and a Swallow (being a bird famous for providence and foresight) called a company of little birds about her, and bad 'em take good notice what that fellow was a doing. You must know (says the Swallow) that all the fowlers' nets and snares are made of hemp or flax; and that's the seed that he is now a sowing. Pick it up in time for fear of what may come on't. In short, they put it off, till it took root; and then again, till it was sprung up into the blade. Upon this, the Swallow told 'em once for all, that it was not yet too late to prevent the mischief, if they would but bestir themselves, and set heartily about it; but finding that no heed was given to what she said, she e'en bad adieu to her old companions in the woods, and so betook herself to a city life, and to the conversation of men. This flax and hemp came in time to be gathered and wrought, and it was this Swallow's fortune to see several of the very same birds that she had forwarned, taken in nets made of the very stuff she told them off. They came at last to be sensible of the folly of slipping their opportunity; but they were lost beyond all redemption first.

15

The Frogs choose a King

IN THE DAYS of old, when the Frogs were all at liberty in the lakes, and grown quite weary of living without government, they petitioned Jupiter for a king, to the end that there might be some distinction of good and evil, by certain equitable rules and methods of reward and punishment. Jupiter, that knew the vanity of their hearts, threw them down a log for their governour; which, upon the first dash, frighted the whole mobile[11] of them into the mud for the very fear on't. This panic terror kept them in awe for a while, till in good time one Frog, bolder than the rest, put up his head, and looked about him to see how squares went with their new king. Upon this, he calls his fellow-subjects together; opens the truth of the case; and nothing would serve them then, but riding a-top of him; insomuch that the dread they were in before, is now turned into insolence and tumult. This king, they said, was too

---

11 Mob.

tame for them, and Jupiter must needs be entreated to send 'em another. He did so, but authors are divided upon it, whether 'twas a stork or a serpent; though whether of the two soever it was, he left them neither liberty nor property, but made a prey of his subjects. Such was their condition in fine, that they sent Mercury to Jupiter yet once again for another king, whose answer was this: They that will not be contented when they are well, must be patient when things are amiss with them; and people had better rest where they are, than go farther and fare worse.

16

A Mountain in Labour

WHEN MOUNTAINS CRY out, people may well be excused the apprehension of some prodigious birth. This was the case here in the fable. The neighbourhood were all at their wits' end to consider what would be the issue of that labour, and instead of the dreadful monster that they expected, out comes at last a ridiculous mouse.

17

The Hares and the Frogs

ONCE UPON A time the Hares found themselves mightily unsatisfied with the miserable condition they lived in, and called a council to advise upon't. Here we live, says one of 'em, at the mercy of men, dogs, eagles, and I know not how many other creatures and vermin, that prey upon us at pleasure; perpetually in frights, perpetually in danger; and therefore I am absolutely of opinion that we had better die once for all, than live at this rate in a continual dread that's worse than death itself. The motion was seconded and debated, and a resolution immediately taken, one and all to drown themselves. The vote was no sooner passed, but away they scudded with that determination to the next river. Upon this hurry, there leapt a whole shoal of frogs from the bank into the water, for fear of the Hares. Nay, then my masters, says one of the gravest of the company, pray let's have a little patience. Our condition I find is not altogether so bad as we fancied it; for there are those you see that are as much afraid of us as we are of others.

18

A Fox and a Stork

THERE WAS A great friendship once betwixt a Fox and a Stork, and the former would needs invite the other to a treat. They had several soups served up in broad dishes and plates, and so the Fox fell to lapping himself, and bade his guest heartily welcome to what was before him. The Stork found he was put upon, but set so good a face however upon his entertainment, that his friend by all means must take a supper with him that night in revenge. The Fox made several excuses upon the matter of trouble and expense, but the Stork in fine would not be said nay; so that at last he promised him to come. The collation was served up in glasses, with long narrow necks, and the best of everything that was to be had. Come (says the Stork to his friend) pray be as free as if you were at home, and so fell to't very savourly himself. The Fox quickly found this to be a trick, though he could not but allow of the contrivance as well as the justice of the revenge. For such a glass of sweet-meats to the one, was just as much to the purpose as a plate of porridge to the other.

19

A Daw and Borrowed Feathers

A DAW THAT had a mind to be sparkish, tricked himself up with all the gay feathers he could muster together. And upon the credit of these stolen or borrowed ornaments, he valued himself above all the birds in the air beside. The pride of this vanity got him the envy of all his companions, who, upon a discovery of the truth of the case, fell to pluming of him by consent; and when every bird had taken his own feather, the silly Daw had nothing left him to cover his nakedness.

20

A Frog and an Ox

AS A HUGE over-grown Ox was grazing in a meadow, an old envious Frog that stood gaping at him hard by, called out to her little ones to take notice of the bulk of that monstrous beast; and see, says she, if I don't make myself now the bigger of the two. So she strained once, and twice, and went still swelling on and on, till in the conclusion she forced herself, and burst.

21

A Horse and a Lion

THERE WAS AN old hungry Lion would fain have been dealing with a piece of good horse-flesh that he had in his eye; but the Nag he thought would be too fleet for him, unless he could supply the want of heels by artifice and address. He imitates the ways and habits of a professor of physic, and according to the humour of the world, sets up for a doctor of the college. Under this pretext, he lets fall a word or two by way of discourse, upon the subject of his trade; but the Horse smelt him out, and presently a crotchet came in his head how he might countermine him. I got a thorn in my foot t'other day, says the Horse, as I was crossing a thicket, and I am e'en quite lame on't. Oh, says the new physician, do but hold up your leg a little, and I'll cure ye immediately. The Lion presently puts himself in posture for the office; but the patient was too nimble for his doctor, and so soon as ever he had him fair for his purpose, gave him so terrible a rebuke upon the forehead with his heel, that he laid him at his length, and so got off with a whole skin, before the other could execute his design.

22

A Bat and a Weasel

A WEASEL HAD seized upon a Bat, and the Bat begged for life. No, no, says the Weasel, I give no quarter to birds. Ay (says the Bat) but I'm a mouse you see; look on my body else. And so she got off for that bout. The same Bat had the fortune to be taken a while after by another weasel; and there the poor Bat was forced to beg for mercy once again. No, says the Weasel, no mercy to a mouse. Well (says t'other) but you may see by my wings that I'm a bird; and so the Bat scaped in both capacities, by playing the trimmer.[12]

---

12 A person who alters his opinions on the grounds of expediency.

23

A Bat, Birds, and Beasts

UPON A DESPERATE and a doubtful battle betwixt the Birds and the Beasts, the Bat stood neuter, till she found that the Beasts had the better on't, and then went over to the stronger side. But it came to pass afterward (as the chance of war is various) that the Birds rallied their broken troops, and carried the day; and away she went then to t'other party, where she was tried by a council of war as a deserter; stripped, banished, and finally condemned never to see daylight again.

24

A Stag Drinking

AS A STAG was drinking upon the bank of a clear stream, he saw his image in the water, and entered into this contemplation upon't. Well! says he, if these pitiful shanks of mine were but answerable to this branching head, I can but think how I should defy all my enemies. The words were hardly out of his mouth, but he discovered a pack of dogs coming full-cry towards him. Away he scours cross the fields, casts off the dogs, and gains a wood; but pressing through a thicket, the bushes held him by the horns, till the hounds came in, and plucked him down. The last thing he said was this: What an unhappy fool was I, to take my friends for my enemies, and my enemies for my friends! I trusted to my head, that has betrayed me, and I found fault with my legs, that would otherwise have brought me off.

25

A League betwixt the Wolves and the Sheep

THERE WAS A time when the Sheep were so hardy as to wage war with the Wolves; and so long as they had the dogs for their allies, they were upon all encounters, at least a match for their enemies. Upon this consideration, the Wolves sent their ambassadors to the Sheep, to treat about a peace, and in the mean time there were hostages given on both sides; the dogs on the part of the Sheep, and the Wolves' whelps on the other part, till matters might be brought to an issue. While they were upon treaty, the whelps fell a howling; the Wolves cried out Treason; and pretending an infraction in the abuse of their hostages, fell upon the Sheep immediately without their dogs, and made them pay for the improvidence of leaving themselves without a guard.

26

An Axe and a Forest

A CARPENTER THAT had got the iron-work of an Axe already, went to the next forest to beg only as much wood as would make a handle to't. The matter seemed so small that the request was easily granted; but when the timber trees came to find that the whole wood was to be cut down by the help of this handle: There's no remedy, they cried, but patience, when people are undone by their own folly.

27

The Eagle and Arrow

AN EAGLE THAT was watching upon a rock once for a hare had the ill hap to be struck with an arrow. This arrow, it seems, was feathered from her own wing, which very consideration went nearer her heart, she said, than death itself.

28

The Belly and Members

THE COMMONERS OF Rome were gone off once into a direct faction against the Senate. They'd pay no taxes, nor be forced to bear arms, they said, and 'twas against the liberty of the subject to pretend to compel them to't. The sedition, in short, ran so high, that there was no hope of reclaiming them, till Menenius Agrippa brought them to their wits again by this apologue:

The hands and the feet were in a desperate mutiny once against the belly. They knew no reason, they said, why the one should be lazying, and pampering itself with the fruit of the other's labour; and if the body would not work for company, they'd be no longer at the charge of maintaining it. Upon this mutiny, they kept the body so long without nourishment, that all the parts suffered for't: insomuch that the hands and feet came in the conclusion to find their mistake, and would have been willing then to have done their office; but it was now too late, for the body was so pined with over-fasting, that it was wholly out of condition to receive the benefit of a relief: which gave them to understand, that body and members are to live and die together.

29

A Lark and her Young Ones

THERE WAS A brood of young Larks in the corn, and the dam, when she went abroad to forage for them, laid a strict charge upon her little ones, to pick up what news they could get against when she came back again. They told her at her return, that the owner of the field had been there, and ordered his neighbours to come and reap the corn. Well, says the old one, there's no danger yet then. They told her the next day that he had been there again, and desired his friends to do't. Well, well, says she, there's no hurt in that neither, and so she went out progging for provisions again as before. But upon the third day, when they told their mother, that the master and his son appointed to come next morning and do't themselves: Nay then, says she, 'tis time to look about us: as for the neighbours and the friends, I fear 'em not; but the master I'm sure will be as good as his word; for 'tis his own business.

30

The Stag and the Oxen

A STAG THAT was hard set by the huntsmen, betook himself to a stall for sanctuary, and prevailed with the Oxen to conceal him the best they could, so they covered him with straw, and by and by in comes the keeper to dress the cattle, and to feed them; and when he had done his work he went his way without any discovery. The Stag reckoned himself by this time to be out of all danger; but one of the Oxen that had more brains than his fellows, advised him not to be too confident neither; for the servant, says he, is a puzzling fool that heeds nothing; but when my master comes, he'll have an eye here and there and every where, and will most certainly find ye out. Upon the very speaking of the word, in comes the master, and he spies out twenty faults, I warrant ye; this was not well, and that was not well; till at last, as he was prying and groping up and down, he felt the horns of the Stag under the straw, and so made prize of him.

31

A Fox and a Sick Lion

A CERTAIN LION that had got a politic fit of sickness, made it his observation, that of all the beasts in the forest, the Fox never came at him. And so he wrote him word how ill he was, and how mighty glad he should be of his company, upon the score of ancient friendship and acquaintance. The Fox returned the compliment with a thousand prayers for his recovery; but as for waiting upon him, he desired to be excused: For (says he) I find the traces of abundance of feet going in to your Majesty's palace, and not one that comes back again.

32

A Boar and a Horse

A BOAR HAPPENED to be wallowing in the water where a Horse was going to drink, and there grew a quarrel upon't. The Horse went presently to a man to assist him in his revenge. They agreed upon the conditions, and the man immediately armed himself, and mounted the Horse, who carried him to the Boar, and had the satisfaction of seeing his enemy killed before his face. The Horse thanked the cavalier for his kindness, but as he was just about to take leave, the man said he should have further occasion for him, and so ordered him to be tied up in the stable. The Horse came by this time to understand that his liberty was gone, and no help for't, and that he had paid dear for his revenge.

33

A Cat and Venus

A YOUNG FELLOW that was passionately in love with a Cat, made it his humble suit to Venus to turn puss into a woman. The transformation was wrought in the twinkling of an eye, and out she comes, a very buxom lass. The doting sot took her home. But a toy took Venus in the head, to try if the Cat had changed her manners with her shape; and so for experiment, turned a mouse loose into the chamber. Madam upon this temptation started out of the bed, and made a leap at the mouse; which Venus took for so high an affront, that she turned the madam into a puss again.

34

A Father and his Sons 1

IT WAS THE hap of a very honest man to be the Father of a contentious brood of children. He called for a birch, and bad 'em take it and try one after another with all their force if they could break it. They tried and could not. Well (says he) unbind it now, and take every twig of it apart, and see what you can do that way. They did so, and with great ease, by one and one, they snapped it all to pieces. This (says he) is the true emblem of your condition. Keep together and y'are safe; divide, and y'are undone.

35

A Trumpeter taken Prisoner

UPON THE ROUT of an army there was a Trumpeter made a prisoner, and as the soldiers were about to cut his throat: Gentlemen (says he), why should you kill a man that kills nobody? You shall die the rather for that, cried one of the company, for being so mean a rascal, as to set other people together by the ears without fighting yourself.

36

A Dog and a Wolf

THERE WAS A hagged carrion of a Wolf and a jolly sort of a Dog, with good flesh upon's back, that fell into company together upon the king's highway. The Wolf was wonderfully pleased with his companion, and as inquisitive to learn how he brought himself to that blessed state of body. Why, says the Dog, I keep my master's house from thieves, and I have very good meat, drink, and lodging for my pains. Now if you'll go along with me and do as I do, you may fare as I fare. The Wolf struck up the bargain, and so away they trotted together. But as they were jogging on, the Wolf spied a bare place about the Dog's neck, where the hair was worn off. Brother (says he) how comes this I prithee? Oh, that's nothing, says the Dog, but the fretting of my collar a little. Nay, says t'other, if there be a collar in the case, I know better things than to sell my liberty for a crust.

37

A Camel at First Sight

UPON THE FIRST sight of a Camel, all people ran away from't, in amazement at so monstrous a bulk. Upon the second sight, finding that it did them no hurt, they took heart upon't, went up to't, and viewed it. But when they came, upon further experience, to take notice how stupid a beast it was, they tied it up, bridled it, loaded it with packs and burthens; set boys upon the back on't, and treated it with the last degree of contempt.

38

A Husbandman and a Stork

A POOR INNOCENT Stork had the ill hap to be taken in a net that was laid for geese and cranes. The Stork's plea for herself was simplicity, and piety: the Love she bore to mankind, and the service she did in picking up of venomous creatures. This is all true, says the Husbandman; but they that keep ill company, if they be caught with ill company, must expect to suffer with ill company.

39

A Boy and False Alarms

A SHEPHERD'S BOY had gotten a roguy trick of crying A wolf, a wolf, when there was no such matter, and fooling the country people with false alarms. He had been at this sport so many times in jest, that they would not believe him at last when he was in earnest: and so the wolves broke in upon the flock, and worried the sheep at pleasure.

40

An Eagle and a Daw

AN EAGLE MADE a stoop at a lamb; trussed it, and took it cleverly away with her. A mimical Daw, that saw this exploit, would needs try the same experiment upon a ram: but his claws were so shackled in the fleece with lugging to get him up, that the shepherd came in and caught him, before he could clear himself; he clipt his wings, and carried him home to his children to play withal. They came gaping about him, and asked their father what strange bird that was? Why, says he, he'll tell you himself that he's an eagle; but if you'll take my word for't, I know him to be a Daw.

41

A Dog in a Manger

A CHURLISH ENVIOUS cur was gotten into a manger, and there lay growling and snarling to keep the horses from their provender. The Dog ate none himself, and yet rather ventured the starving of his own carcase than he would suffer any thing else to be the better for't.

42

A Peacock to Juno

THE PEACOCK, THEY say, laid it extremely to heart, that being Juno's darling-bird, he had not the nightingale's voice superadded to the beauty of his own plumes. Upon this subject he petitioned his patroness, who gave him for answer, that providence had assigned every bird its proportion, and so bade him content himself with his lot.

43

A Fox and a Goat

A FOX AND a Goat went down by consent into a well to drink, and when they had quenched their thirst, the Goat fell to hunting up and down which way to get back again. Oh! says Reynard, never trouble your head how to get back, but leave that to me. Do but you raise yourself upon your hinder legs with your fore-feet close to the wall, and then stretch out your head: I can easily whip up to your horns, and so out of the well and draw you after me. The Goat puts himself in a posture immediately as he was directed, gives the Fox a lift, and so out he springs; but Reynard's business was now only to make sport with his companion instead of helping him. Some hard words the Goat gave him, but the Fox puts off all with a jest. If you had but half so much brain as beard, says he, you would have bethought yourself how to get up again before you went down.

44

A Bragging Traveller

A VAIN FELLOW that had been abroad in the world would still be tiring all people's ears at his return, with stories of his wonderful actions and adventures in his travels; and particularly he told of a leap he took at Rhodes, that nobody there could come within six foot on't. Now this (says he) I am able to prove by several witnesses upon the place. If this be true (says one of the company) there's no need of going to Rhodes for witnesses: do but you fancy this to be Rhodes, and then shew us the leap.

45

A Woman and a Fat Hen

A GOOD WOMAN had a Hen that laid her every day an egg. Now she fancied to herself, that upon a larger allowance of corn, this Hen might be brought in time to lay twice a day. She tried the experiment; but the hen grew fat upon't and gave quite over laying.

46

A Man bit by a Dog

ONE THAT WAS bitten by a Dog was advised, as the best remedy in the world, to dip a piece of bread in the blood of the wound, and give it the Dog to eat. Pray hold your hand a little (says the Man) unless y'ave a mind to draw all the dogs in the town upon me; for that will certainly be the end on't, when they shall find themselves rewarded instead of punished.

47

Two Enemies at Sea

THERE WERE TWO Enemies at Sea in the same vessel, the one at the ship's head, the other at the stern. It blew a dreadful storm, and when the vessel was just ready to be swallowed up, one of 'em asked the master, which part of the ship would be first under water; so he told him t'other end would sink first. Why then, says he, I shall have the comfort of seeing my enemy go before me.

48

A Fortune Teller

THERE WAS A kind of a petty Conjurer, that made it his profession to resolve questions, and tell fortunes, and he held forth in the market-place. Word was brought him, 'in the very middle of his schemes and calculations, that his house was robbed; and so away he scours immediately to learn the truth on't. As he was running home in all haste, a droll takes him up by the way with this short question. Friend (says he) how came you to be so good at telling other people's fortunes, and know so little of your own?

49

An Astrologer and a Traveller

A CERTAIN STAR-gazer had the fortune, in the very height of his celestial observations, to stumble into a ditch; a sober fellow passing by, gave him a piece of wholesome counsel. Friend, says he, make a right use of your present misfortune and pray, for the future, let the stars go on quietly in their courses, and do you look a little better to the ditches.

50

A Shepherd turned Merchant

A COUNTRYMAN WAS feeding his flock by the seaside, and it was so delicate a fine day, that the smoothness of the water tempted him to leave his shepherd's business, and set up for a Merchant. So that in all haste, he puts off his stock; buys a bargain of figs; gets his freight aboard, and away presently to sea. It happened to be very foul weather; so that the mariners were fain to cast their whole lading overboard, to save themselves and the vessel. Upon this miscarriage, our new merchant-adventurer betook himself to his old trade again; and it happened one day, as he was tending his sheep upon the very same coast, to be just such a flattering tempting sea again, as that which betrayed him before. Yes, yes, says he, when the Devil's blind! You'd ha' some more figs, with a vengeance, would ye?

51

The Fox that lost his Tail

THERE WAS A Fox taken in a trap, that was glad to compound for his neck by leaving his tail behind him. It was so uncouth a sight for a Fox to appear without a tail, that the very thought on't made him e'en weary of his life; for 'twas a loss never to be repaired. But however for the better countenance of the scandal, he got the Master and Wardens of the Foxes Company to call a Court of Assistants, where he himself appeared, and made a learned discourse upon the trouble, the uselessness, and the indecency of Foxes wearing tails. He had no sooner said out his say, but up rises a cunning snap, then at the board, who desired to be informed whether the worthy member that moved against the wearing of tails gave his advice for the advantage of those that had tails, or to palliate the deformity and disgrace of those that had none.

52

A Fox and Huntsmen

A FOX THAT had been hard-run begged of a countryman that he saw at work in a wood to help him to some hiding-place. The man directed him to his cottage, and thither he went. He was no sooner got in, but the Huntsmen were presently at the heels of him, and asked the cottager if he did not see a fox that way? No truly, says he, I saw none; but pointed at the same time with his finger to the place where he lay. The Huntsmen did not take the hint, it seems; but the Fox spied him, however, through a peeping-hole he had found out to see what news; so the fox-hunters went their way, and then out steals the Fox, without one word speaking. Why how now, says the man, han't ye the manners to take leave of your host before you go? Yes, yes, says the Fox; if you had been as honest of your fingers as you were of your tongue, I should not have gone without bidding ye farewell.

53

A Father and his Sons 2

A COUNTRYMAN THAT lived handsomely in the world himself, upon his honest labour and industry, was desirous his sons should do so after him; and being now upon his death-bed: My dear children (says he) I reckon myself bound to tell you before I depart, that there is a considerable treasure hid in my vineyard. Wherefore pray be sure to dig, and search narrowly for't when I am gone. The father dies, and the sons fall immediately to work upon the vineyard. They turned it up over and over, and not one penny of money to be found there; but the profit of the next vintage expounded the riddle.

54

A Fisherman and his Pipe

A FISHERMAN THAT understood piping better than netting, set himself down upon the side of a river, and touched his flute, but not a fish came near him. Upon this, he laid down his pipe and cast his net, which brought him up a very great draught. The fish fell a frisking in the net, and the Fisherman observing it: What sots are these (says he) that would not dance when I played to 'em, and will be dancing now without music!

55

Large Promises

THERE WAS A poor sick man, that according to the course of the world, when physicians had given him over, betook himself to his prayers, and vowed a sacrifice of a thousand oxen ready down upon the nail, to either Apollo or Æsculapius, which of the two would deliver him from this disease. Ah my dear (says his wife), have a care what you promise; for where would you have these oxen if you should recover? Sweetheart (says he), thou talkest like a fool. Have the Gods nothing else to do, dost think, than to leave their business, and come down to sue me in action of debt? They restored him however for that bout, to make trial of his honesty and good faith. He was no sooner up, but for want of living oxen, he made out his number upon paste, and offered them up in form upon an altar. For this mockery, divine vengeance pursued him, and he had an apparition came to him in a dream, that bade him go and search in such a place near the coast, and he should find a considerable treasure; away he went, and as he was looking for the money fell into the hands of pirates. He begged hard for his liberty, and offered a thousand talents of gold for his ransom; but they would not trust him, and so he was carried away, and sold afterwards as a slave for as many groats.

56

Death and an Old Man

AN OLD MAN that had travelled a great way under a huge burden of sticks found himself so weary, that he cast it down and called upon Death to deliver him from a more miserable life. Death came presently at his call, and asked him his business. Pray good sir, says he, do me but the favour to help me up with my burden again.

57

A Doctor and Patient with Sore Eyes

A PHYSICIAN UNDERTAKES a woman with sore eyes, upon the terms of no cure no money. His way was to daub 'em quite up with ointments, and while she was in that pickle, to carry off a spoon or a porringer,[13] or somewhat or other, at the end of his visit. The woman's eyes mended, and still as she came more and more to herself again, there was every day less and less left in the house to be seen. The doctor came to her at last, and told her: Mistress, says he, I have discharged my part, your eyes are perfectly well again, and pray let me be paid now according to our agreement. Alas, sir, says she, I'm a great deal worse than I was the first minute you undertook me; for I could see plate, hangings, paintings, and other goods of value about my house, 'till you had the ordering of me; but I am now brought to such a pass, that I can see nothing at all.

---

13 A small dish

58

An Ape and a Fox

UPON THE DECEASE of a lion of late famous memory, the beasts met in council to choose a king. There were several put up; but one was not of a make for a king, another wanted either brains, or strength, or stature, or humour, or something else; but in fine, the Buffoon-Ape, with his grimaces and gambols, carried it from the whole field by I know not how many voices. The Fox (being one of the pretenders) stomached it[14] extremely to see the choice go against him, and presently rounds the new-elect in the ear, with a piece of secret service that he could do him. Sir, says he, I have discovered some hidden treasure yonder; but 'tis a royalty that belongs to your Majesty, and I have nothing to do with it. So he carried the Ape to take possession; and what should this treasure be, but a bait in a ditch. The Ape lays his hand upon't, and the trap springs and catches him by the fingers. Ah thou perfidious wretch, cries the Ape. Or thou simple Prince, rather, replies the Fox. You a governor of others, with a vengeance, that han't wit enough to look to your own fingers.

---

14 Was angry.

59

A Dog and a Wolf

A WOLF TOOK a Dog napping at his master's door, and when he was just about to worry him, the poor creature begged hard only for a reprieve. Alas (says he) I'm as lean at present as carrion; but we have a wedding at our house within these two or three days, that will plump me up you shall see with good cheer. Pray have but patience till then, and when I'm in a little better case, I'll throw myself in the very mouth of ye. The Wolf took his word, and so let him go; but passing some few days after by the same house again, he spied the Dog in the hall, and bade him remember his promise. Hark ye, my friend, says the Dog: whenever you catch me asleep again on the wrong side of the door never trouble your head to wait for a wedding.

60

A Lion and a Bull

IN THE DAYS of yore, when Bulls lived upon mutton, there was a Lion had a design upon a mighty Bull, and gave him a very civil invitation to come and sup with him; for, says he, I have gotten a sheep, and you must needs take part on't. The Bull promised, and went; but so soon as ever he saw what a clutter there was with huge, over-grown pots, pans, and spits, away he scoured immediately. The Lion presently called after him, and asked him, Whither in such haste? Oh, says the Bull, 'tis high time for me to be jogging, when I see such preparation; for this provision looks as if you were to have a Bull for your supper, rather than a mutton.

61

A Lion in Love

A LION FELL in love with a country lass, and desired her father's consent to have her in marriage. The answer he gave was churlish enough. He'd never agree to't he said, upon any terms, to marry his daughter to a beast. The Lion gave him a sour look upon't, which brought the bumpkin, upon second thoughts, to strike up a bargain with him, upon these conditions: that his teeth should be drawn, and his nails pared; for those were things, he said, that the foolish girl was terribly afraid of. The Lion sends for a surgeon immediately to do the work (as what will not love make a body do?). And so soon as ever the operation was over, he goes and challenges the father upon his promise. The countryman seeing the Lion disarmed, plucked up a good heart, and with a swinging cudgel so ordered the matter, that he broke off the match.

62

A Fawn and a Stag

A FAWN WAS reasoning the matter with a Stag, why he should run away from the dogs still; for, says he, you are bigger and stronger than they. If you have a mind to stand, y'are better armed; and then y'are fleeter if you'll run for't. I can't imagine what should make you so fearful of a company of pitiful curs. Nay, says the Stag, 'tis all true that you say, and 'tis no more than I say to myself many times, and yet whatever the matter is, let me take up what resolutions I please, when I hear the hounds once, I cannot but betake myself to my heels.

63

Jupiter and a Bee

A BEE MADE Jupiter a present of a pot of honey, which was so kindly taken, that he bade her ask what she would, and it should be granted her. The Bee desired, that wherever she should set her sting it might be mortal. Jupiter was loth to leave mankind at the mercy of a little spiteful insect, and so bade her have a care how she killed anybody; for what person soever she attacked, if she left her sting behind her, it should cost her her life.

64

Mercury and a Carpenter

A CARPENTER DROPPED his axe into a river, and put up a prayer to Mercury to help him to't again. Mercury dived for't, and brought him up a golden one: but that was not it the fellow said; and so he plunged a second time, and fetched up another, of silver. He said that was not it either. He tried once again, and then up comes an axe with a wooden handle, which the Carpenter said was the very tool that he had lost. Well! (says Mercury) thou art so just a poor wretch, that I'll give thee all three now for thy honesty. This story was got into everybody's mouth, and the rumour being spread, it came into a knave's head to try the same experiment over again. And so away goes he and down he sits, snivelling and yelping upon the bank of a river, that he had dropped his axe into the water there. Mercury that was at hand, it seems, heard his lamentation, and dipping once again for his axe, as he had done for the other, up he brings him a golden axe, and asks the fellow if that were it. Yes, yes, says he, this is it. Oh thou impudent sot, cries Mercury; to think of putting tricks upon him that sees through the very heart of thee.

65

A Fox and Grapes

THERE WAS A time when a Fox would have ventured as far for a bunch of grapes as for a shoulder of mutton; and it was a Fox of those days, and that palate, that stood gaping under a vine, and licking his lips at a most delicious cluster of grapes that he had spied out there. He fetched a hundred and a hundred leaps at it, till at last, when he was as weary as a dog, and found that there was no good to be done: Hang 'em (says he) they are as sour as crabs;[15] and so away he went, turning off the disappointment with a jest.

---

15 Crab-apples.

66

A Wolf and a Lion

AS A WOLF and a Lion were abroad upon adventure together: Hark! (says the Wolf), don't you hear the bleating of sheep? My life for yours, sir, I'll go fetch you a purchase. Away he goes, and follows his ear till he came just under the sheepfold; but it was so well fortified, and the dogs asleep so near it, that back he came sneaking to the Lion again, and tells him: There are sheep yonder (says he) 'tis true, but they are as lean as carrion, and we had e'en as good let 'em alone till they have more flesh on their backs.

67

A Hare and a Tortoise

WHAT A DULL heavy creature (says a Hare) is this same Tortoise! And yet (says the Tortoise) I'll run with you for a wager. 'Twas done and done, and the Fox, by consent, was to be the judge. They started together, and the Tortoise kept jogging on still, 'till he came to the end of the course. The Hare laid himself down about mid-way and took a nap; for, says he, I can fetch up the Tortoise when I please. But he over-slept himself it seems, for when he came to wake, though he scudded away as fast as 'twas possible, the Tortoise got to the post before him, and won the wager.

68

A Man and Two Wives

IT WAS NOW cuckoo-time, and a certain middle-aged man, that was half-gray, half-brown, took a fancy to marry two wives, of an age one under another, and happy was the woman that could please him best. They took mighty care of him to all manner of purposes, and still as they were combing the good man's head, they'd be picking out here and there a hair to make it all of a colour. The matronly wife, she plucked out all the brown hairs, and the younger the white; so that they left the man in the conclusion no better than a bald buzzard betwixt them.

69

Two Frogs that wanted Water

UPON THE DRYING up of a lake, two Frogs were forced to quit, and to seek for water elsewhere. As they were upon the search, they discovered a very deep well. Come (says one to t'other) let us e'en go down here, without looking any further. You say well, says her companion; but what if the water should fail us here too? How shall we get out again?

70

A Bat, Bramble, and Cormorant

A Bat, a Bramble, and a Cormorant entered into covenants with articles, to join stocks, and trade in partnership together. The Bat's adventure was ready money that he took up at interest; the Bramble's was in clothes; and the Cormorant's in brass. They put to sea, and it so fell out, that ship and goods were both lost by stress of weather. But the three merchants by providence got safe to land. Since the time of this miscarriage, the Bat never stirs abroad till night, for fear of his creditors. The Bramble lays hold of all the clothes he can come at in hope to light upon his own again; and the Cormorant is still sauntering by the seaside, to see if he can find any of his brass cast up.

71

A Miser burying his Gold

A CERTAIN COVETOUS, rich churl sold his whole estate, and put it into money, and then melted down that money again into one mass, which he buried in the ground, with his very heart and soul in the pot for company. He gave it a visit every morning, which it seems was taken notice of, and somebody that observed him found out his hoard one night, and carried it away. The next day he missed it, and ran almost out of his wits for the loss of his gold. Well (says a neighbour to him), and what's all this rage for? Why you had no gold at all, and so you lost none. You did but fancy all this while that you had it, and you may e'en as well fancy again that you have it still. 'Tis but laying a stone where you laid your money, and fancying that stone to be your treasure, and there's your gold again. You did not use it when you had it; and you do not want it so long as you resolve not to use it.

72

A Stag with One Eye

A ONE-EYED STAG that was afraid of the huntsmen at land, kept a watch that way with t'other eye, and fed with his blind side still towards an arm of the sea, where he thought there was no danger. In this prospect of security, he was struck with an arrow from a boat, and so ended his days with this lamentation: Here am I destroyed, says he, where I reckoned myself to be safe on the one hand; and no evil has befallen me, where I most dreaded it, on the other.

73

A Goat and a Vine

A GOAT THAT was hard pressed by the huntsmen took sanctuary in a vineyard, and there he lay close, under the covert of a vine. So soon as he thought the danger was over, he fell presently to browsing upon the leaves; and whether it was the rustling, or the motion of the boughs, that gave the huntsmen an occasion for a stricter search, is uncertain; but a search there was, and in the end he was discovered, and shot. He died in fine, with this conviction upon him, that his punishment was just, for offering violence to his protector.

74

A Gardener and his Dog

A GARDENER'S DOG dropped into a well, and his master let himself down to help him out again. He reached forth his hand to take hold of the Dog, and the cur snapt him by the fingers: for he thought 'twas only to duck him deeper. The master went his way upon't, and e'en left him as he found him. Nay (says he), I'm well enough served, to take so much pains for the saving of one that is resolved to make away himself.

75

A Snake and a Crab

THERE WAS A familiarity contracted betwixt a Snake and a Crab. The Crab was a plain dealing creature, that advised his companion to give over shuffling and doubling, and to practice good faith. The Snake went on in his old way: so that the Crab finding that he would not mend his manners, set upon him in his sleep, and strangled him; and then looking upon him as he lay dead at his length: This had never befall'n ye, says he, if you had but lived as straight as you died.

76

A Lion, Fox, and a Wolf

THE KING OF beasts was now grown old and sickly, and all his subjects of the forest (saving only the Fox) were to pay their duties to him. The Wolf and the Fox like a couple of sly knaves, were still putting tricks one upon another, and the Wolf took this occasion to do the Fox a good office. I can assure your Majesty, says the Wolf, that 'tis nothing but pride and insolence that keeps the Fox from shewing himself at court as well as his companions. Now the Fox had the good luck to be within hearing, and so presented himself before the Lion, and finding him extremely enraged, begs his Majesty's patience, and a little time only for his defence. Sir (says he), I must presume to value myself upon my respect and loyalty to your Majesty, equal at least to any of your other subjects; and I will be bold to say, that put them all together, they have not taken half the pains for your Majesty's service now upon this very occasion that I have done. I have been hunting up and down far and near, since your unhappy indisposition, to find out a remedy for ye, which with much ado I have now compassed at last, and it is that which I promised myself will prove an infallible cure. Tell me immediately (says the Lion) what it is then. Nothing in the world, says the Fox, but to slay a Wolf alive, and wrap your body up in the warm skin. The Wolf was by all this while; and the Fox in a sneering way advised him for the future not to irritate a Prince against his subjects, but rather to sweeten him with peaceable and healing counsels.

77

Two Travellers and a Bag of Money

AS TWO TRAVELLERS were upon the way together, one of 'em stoops and takes up something. Look ye here (says he), I have found a bag of money. No, says t'other, when two friends are together, you must not say I have found it, but We have found it. The word was no sooner out, but immediately comes a hue and cry after a gang of thieves that had taken a purse upon the road. Lord! brother (says he that had the bag) we shall be utterly undone. Oh fie, says t'other, you must not say We shall be undone, but I shall be undone; for if I'm to have no part in the finding, sure I'll never go halves in the hanging.

78

Fishing in Troubled Waters

A FISHERMAN HAD ordered his net for a draught, and still as he was gathering it up he dashed the water, to fright the fish into the Bag. Some of the neighbourhood that looked on told him he did ill to muddle the water so, and spoil their drink. Well (says he), but I must either spoil your drink, or have nothing to eat myself.

79

An Ape and a Dolphin

PEOPLE WERE USED in the days of old to carry gamesome puppies and apes with 'em to sea, to pass away the time withal. Now there was one of these apes, it seems, aboard a vessel that was cast away in a very great storm. As the men were paddling for their lives, and the Ape for company, a certain Dolphin that took him for a man got him upon his back, and was making towards land with him. He had him into a safe road[16] called the Piræus, and took occasion to ask the Ape, whether he was an Athenian or not? He told him Yes, and of a very ancient family there. Why then (says the Dolphin) you know Piræus. Oh! exceedingly well, says t'other (taking it for the name of a man). Why Piræus is my very particular good friend. The Dolphin, upon this, had such an indignation for the impudence of the buffoon-ape, that he gave him the slip from between his legs, and there was an end of my very good friend, the Athenian.

---

16 Roadstead, harbour.

80

Mercury and a Statuary

MERCURY HAD A great mind once to learn what credit he had in the world, and he knew no better way than to put on the shape of a man, and take occasion to discourse the matter as by the by, with a Statuary; so away he went to the house of a great master, where, among other curious figures, he saw several excellent pieces of the Gods. The first he cheapened was a Jupiter, which would have come at a very easy rate. Well (says Mercury) and what's the price of that Juno there? The carver set that a little higher. The next figure was a Mercury, with his rod and his wings, and all the ensigns of his commission. Why, this is as it should be, says he, to himself: for here am I in the quality of Jupiter's messenger, and the patron of artisans, with all my trade about me: and now will this fellow ask me fifteen times as much for this as he did for t'other; and so he put it to him, what he valued that piece at: Why truly, says the Statuary, you seem to be a civil gentleman, give me but my price for the other two, and you shall e'en have that into the bargain.

81

A Hound and a Mastiff

THERE WAS A man had two dogs; one for the chase. t'other to look to the house; and whatever the Hound took abroad, the house-dog had his part on't at home. T'other grumbled at it, that when he took all the pains the Mastiff should reap the fruit of his labours. Well, says the house-dog, that's none of my fault, but my master's, that has not trained me up to work for myself, but to eat what others have provided for me.

82

A Wolf and a Kid

A WOLF SPIED out a straggling Kid, and pursued him. The Kid found that the Wolf was too nimble for him, and so turned and told him: I perceive I am to be eaten, and I would gladly die as pleasantly as I could; wherefore, pray give me but one touch of your pipe before I go to pot. The Wolf played and the Kid danced, and the noise of the pipe brought in the dogs upon him. Well (says the Wolf) this 'tis when people will be meddling out of their profession. My business was to play the butcher, not the piper.

83

Thieves that stole a Cock

A BAND OF Thieves brake into a house once, and found nothing in't to carry away but one poor Cock. The Cock said as much for himself as a Cock could say; but insisted chiefly upon the services of his calling people up to their work, when 'twas time to rise. Sirrah (says one of the Thieves) you had better have let that argument alone; for your waking the family spoils our trade, and we are to be hanged forsooth for your bawling.

84

A Crow and a Raven

YOUR RAVEN HAS a reputation in the world for a bird of omen, and a kind of small prophet. A Crow that had observed the Raven's manner and way of delivering his predictions, sets up for a foreboder too; and so gets upon a tree, and there stands nodding and croaking, just over the head of some people that were passing by. They were a little surprised at first; but so soon as they saw how 'twas: Come, my masters (says one of the Company) let's e'en go forward, for this is but the chattering of a foolish Crow, and it signifies nothing.

85

A Raven and a Snake

AS A SNAKE lay lazing at his length in the gleam of the sun, a Raven took him up, and flew away with him. The Snake kept a twisting and a turning, till he bit the Raven, and made him curse himself for being such a fool, as to meddle with a purchase that cost him his life.

86

A Daw and Pigeons

A DAW TOOK particular notice of the Pigeons in such a certain dove-house, that they were very well fed, and provided for; so he went and painted himself of a dove colour, and took his commons with the Pigeons. So long as he kept his own counsel, he passed for a bird of the same feather; but it was his hap once at unawares to cry Kaw, upon which discovery, they beat him out of the house, and when he came to his old companions again, they'd have none of him either; so that he lost himself both ways by this disguise.

87

Jupiter's Wedding

WHEN THE TOY had once taken Jupiter in the head to enter into a state of matrimony, he resolved for the honour of his celestial lady, that the whole world should keep a festival upon the day of his marriage, and so invited all living creatures, tag-rag and bob-tail, to the solemnity of his wedding. They all came in very good time, saving only the tortoise. Jupiter told him 'twas ill done to make the company stay, and asked him: Why so late? Why truly, says the tortoise, I was at home, at my own house, my dearly-beloved house, and home is home, let it be never so homely. Jupiter took it very ill at his hands, that he should think himself better in a ditch, than in a palace, and so he passed this judgment upon him; that since he would not be persuaded to come out of his house upon that occasion, he should never stir abroad again from that day forward, without his house upon his head.

88

A Wolf and a Sheep

A WOLF THAT lay licking of his wounds, and extremely faint and ill, upon the biting of a dog, called out to a Sheep that was passing by: Hark ye friend (says he) if thou wouldst but help me to a sup of water out of that same brook there, I could make a shift to get myself somewhat to eat. Yes, says the Sheep, I make no doubt on't; but when I bring ye drink, my carcass shall serve ye for meat to't.

89

A Wild Ass and a Tame

AS A TAME Ass was airing himself in a pleasant meadow, with a coat and carcass in very good plight, up comes a Wild one to him from the next wood, with this short greeting: Brother (says he) I envy your happiness; and so he left him. It was his hap some short time after this encounter, to see his Tame brother, groaning under an unmerciful pack, and a fellow at his heels goading him forward. He rounds him in the ear upon't, and whispers him: My friend (says he) your condition is not, I perceive, what I took it to be, for a body may buy gold too dear: and I am not purchasing good looks and provender at this rate.

90

An Ass and the Frogs

AN ASS SUNK down into a bog among a shoal of Frogs, with a burden of wood upon his back, and there he lay, sighing and groaning, as his heart would break. Hark ye friend (says one of the Frogs to him) if you make such a business of a quagmire, when you are but just fallen into't, what would you do I wonder if you had been here as long as we have been?

91

A Galled Ass and a Raven

AS AN ASS with a galled back was feeding in a meadow, a Raven pitched upon him, and there sat, jobbing of the sore. The Ass fell a frisking, and braying upon't; which set a groom, that saw it at a distance, a laughing at it. Well! (says a wolf that was passing by) to see the injustice of the world now! A poor wolf in that Raven's place would have been persecuted, and hunted to death presently; and 'tis made only a laughing matter, for a Raven to do the same thing that would have cost a wolf his life.

92

An Ass, a Fox, and a Lion

AS AN ASS and a Fox were together upon the ramble, a Lion meets them by the way. The Fox's heart went pit-a-pat; but however to make the best of a bad game, he sets a good face on't, and up he goes to the Lion. Sir, says he, I am come to offer your Majesty a piece of service, and I'll cast myself upon your honour for my own security. If you have a mind to my companion, the Ass here, 'tis but a word speaking, and you shall have him immediately. Let it be done then, says the Lion. So the Fox trepanned the Ass into the toil, and the Lion, when he found he had him sure, began with the Fox himself, and after that, for his second course, made up his meal with the other.

93

Jupiter and a Herdsman

A HERDSMAN THAT had lost a calf out of his grounds, sent up and down after it; and when he could get no tidings on't, he betook himself at last to his prayers, according to the custom of the world, when people are brought to a forced put. Great Jupiter (says he) do but shew me the thief that stole my calf, and I'll give thee a kid for a sacrifice. The word was no sooner passed, but the thief appeared, which was indeed a lion. This discovery put him to his prayers once again. I have not forgotten my vow, says he, but now thou hast brought me to the thief, I'll make that kid a bull, if thou'lt but set me quit of him again.

94

A Gnat challenges a Lion

AS A LION was blustering in the forest, up comes a Gnat to his very beard, and enters into an expostulation with him upon the points of honour and courage. What do I value your teeth, or your claws, says the Gnat, that are but the arms of every bedlam slut? As to' the matter of resolution; I defy ye to put that point immediately to an issue. So the trumpet sounded, and the combatants entered the lists. The Gnat charged into the nostrils of the Lion, and there twinged him, till he made him tear himself with his own paws. And in the conclusion he mastered the Lion. Upon this, a retreat was sounded, and the Gnat flew his way; but by ill-hap afterward, in his flight he struck into a cobweb, where the victor fell a prey to the spider. This disgrace went to the heart of him, after he had got the better of a Lion, to be worsted by an insect.

95

A Peacock and a Pie

IN THE DAYS of old, the birds lived at random in a lawless state of anarchy; but in time they began to be weary on't, and moved for the setting up of a king. The Peacock valued himself upon his gay feathers, and put in for the office. The pretenders were heard, the question debated; and the choice fell upon the poll to king Peacock. The vote was no sooner passed, but up stands a Pie with a speech in his mouth to this effect: May it please your Majesty, says he, we should be glad to know, in case the Eagle should fall upon us in your reign, as she has formerly done, how will you be able to defend us?

96

A Lion, Ass, and Fox

THERE WAS A hunting-match agreed upon betwixt a Lion, an Ass, and a Fox, and they were to go equal shares in the booty. They ran down a brave stag, and the Ass was to divide the prey; which he did very honestly and innocently into three equal parts, and left the Lion to take his choice: Who never minded the dividend; but in a rage worried the Ass, and then bade the Fox divide; who had the wit to make only one share of the whole, saving a miserable pittance that he reserved for himself. The Lion highly approved of his way of distribution; but prithee Reynard, says he, who taught thee to carve? Why truly, says the Fox, I had an Ass to my master; and it was his folly made me wise.

97

A Woman and her Maids

IT WAS THE way of a good housewifely old Woman to call up her Maids every morning just at the cock-crowing. The wenches were loth to rise so soon, and so they laid their heads together, and killed the poor cock: for, say they, if it were not for his waking our dame, she would not wake us; but when the good woman's clock was gone, she'd mistake the hours many times, and call 'em up at midnight; so that instead of mending the matter, they found themselves in a worse condition now than before.

98

A Lion and a Goat

A LION SPIED a Goat upon the crag of a high rock and so called out to him after this manner: Hadst not thou better come down now, says the Lion, into this delicate fine meadow? Well, says the Goat, and so perhaps I would, if it were not for the Lion that's there before me: but I'm for a life of safety, rather than a life of pleasure. Your pretence is the filling of my belly with good grass; but your business is the cramming of your own guts with good goats' flesh: so that 'tis for your own sake, not mine, that you'd have me come down.

99

An Oak and a Willow

THERE HAPPENED A controversy betwixt an Oak and a Willow, upon the subject of strength, constancy, and patience, and which of the two should have the preference. The Oak upbraided the Willow, that it was weak and wavering, and gave way to every blast. The Willow made no other reply, than that the next tempest should resolve that question. Some very little while after this dispute, it blew a violent storm. The Willow plied, and gave way to the gust, and still recovered itself again, without receiving any damage; but the Oak was stubborn, and chose rather to break than bend.

100

An Eagle and an Owl

A CERTAIN EAGLE that had a mind to be well served took up a resolution of preferring those that she found most agreeable, for person and address; and so there past an order of council for all her Majesty's subjects to bring their children to court. They came accordingly, and everyone in their turn was for advancing their own; till at last the Owl fell a mopping, and twinkling, and told her Majesty, that if a gracious mien and countenance might entitle any of her subjects to a preference, she doubted not but her brood would be looked upon in the first place; for they were as like the mother, as if they had been spit out of her mouth. Upon this the board fell into a fit of laughing, and called another cause.

101

An Old Crab and a Young

CHILD (SAYS THE mother), you must use yourself to walk straight, without skewing and shailing so every step you set. Pray mother (says the Young Crab), do but set the example yourself, and I'll follow ye

102

The Goose and Gosling

WHY DO YOU go nodding and waggling so like a fool, as if you were hipshot? says the Goose to her Gosling. The young one tried to mend it, but could not; and so the mother tied little sticks to her legs, to keep her upright; but the little one complained then, that she could neither swim nor dabble with 'em. Well, says the mother, do but hold up your head at least. The Gosling endeavoured to do that too; but upon the stretching out of her long neck, she complained that she could not see the way before her. Nay then, says the Goose, if it will be no better, e'en carry your head and your feet as your elders have done before ye

103

The Sun and the Wind

THE HAPPENED A controversy betwixt the Sun and the Wind, which was the stronger of the two; and they put the point upon this issue: There was a traveller upon the way, and which of the two could make that fellow quit his cloak should carry the cause. The Wind fell presently a storming, and threw hail-shot over and above in the very teeth of him. The man wraps himself up, and keeps advancing still in spite of the weather; but this gust in a short time blew over; and then the Sun brake out, and fell to work upon him with his beams; but still he pushes forward, sweating, and panting, till in the end he was forced to quit his cloak, and lay himself down upon the ground in a cool shade for his relief; so that the Sun, in the conclusion, carried the point.

104

An Ass in a Lion's Skin

THERE WAS A freak[17] took an Ass in the head, to scour abroad upon the ramble; and away he goes into the woods, masquerading up and down in a Lion's skin. The world was his own for a while, and wherever he went, man and beast fled before him; but he had the hap in the conclusion, partly by his voice, and partly by his ears, to be discovered, and consequently uncased, well laughed at, and well cudgelled for his pains.

17 Whim or caprice

105

Two Friends and a Bear

TWO FRIENDS THAT were travelling together had the fortune to meet a Bear upon the way. They found there was no running for't. So the one whips up a tree, and the other throws himself flat with his face upon the ground. The Bear comes directly up to him, muzzles, and smells to him, puts his nose to his mouth, and to his ears, and at last, taking for granted that 'twas only a carcass, there he leaves him. The Bear was no sooner gone, but down comes his companion, and asked him, what it was the Bear whispered him in the ear. He bade me have a care, says he, how I keep company with those that, when they find themselves upon a pinch, will leave their friends in the lurch.

106

A Horseman's Wig blown off

THERE WAS A horseman had a cap on with a false head of hair tacked to't. There comes a puff of wind, and blows off cap and wig together. The people made sport, he saw, with his bald crown, and so very fairly he put in with them to laugh for company. Why gentlemen (says he), would you have me keep other people's hair better than I did my own?

107

Two Pots

THERE WERE TWO Pots that stood near one another by the side of a river, the one of brass, and the other' of clay. The water overflowed the banks, and carried them both away: the earthern vessel kept aloof from t'other, as much as possible. Fear nothing, says the brass pot, I'll do you no hurt: no, no, says t'other, not willingly; but if we should happen to knock by chance, 'twould be the same thing to me: so that you and I shall never do well together.

108

Good Luck and Bad Luck

THERE WAS A middling sort of a man that was left well enough to pass by his father, but could never think he had enough, so long as any man had more. He took notice what huge estates many merchants got in a very short time; and so sold his inheritance, and betook himself to a way of traffic and commerce. Matters succeeded so wonderfully well with him, that everybody was in admiration to see how mighty rich he was grown all on a sudden. Why ay, says he, this 'tis when a man understands his business; for I have done all this by my industry. It would have been well if he had stopped there; but avarice is insatiable, and so he went pushing on still for more; till, what by wrecks, bankrupts, pirates, and I know not how many other disappointments, one upon the neck of another, he was reduced in half the time that he was a rising, to a morsel of bread. Upon these miscarriages, people were at him over and over again, to know how this came about. Why, says he, my fortune would have it so. Fortune happened to be at that time within hearing, and told him in his ear, that he was an arrogant, ungrateful clown, to charge her with all the evil that befell him, and to take the good to himself.

109

A Peacock and a Crane

AS A PEACOCK and a Crane were in company together, the Peacock spreads his tail, and challenges the other to shew him such a fan of feathers. The Crane, upon this, springs up into the air, and calls to the Peacock to follow him if he could. You brag of your plumes, says he, that are fair indeed to the eye, but no way useful or fit for any manner of service.

110

A Fir and a Bramble

THERE GOES A story of a Fir-tree, that in a vain, spiteful humour was mightily upon the pin of commending itself, and despising the Bramble. My head (says the Fir) is advanced among the stars. I furnish beams for palaces, masts for shipping; the very sweat of my body is a sovereign remedy for the sick and wounded; whereas the rascally Bramble runs creeping in the dirt, and serves for no purpose in the world but mischief. Well (says the Bramble, that overheard all this), you might have said somewhat of your own misfortune, and to my advantage too, if your pride and envy would have suffered you to do it. But pray will you tell me, however, when the carpenter comes next with his axe into the wood to fell timber, whether you had not rather be a Bramble than a Fir-tree.

111

A Covetous Man and an Envious

THERE WAS A Covetous and an Envious Man, that joined in a petition to Jupiter, who very graciously ordered Apollo to tell them that their desire should be granted at a venture; provided only, that whatever the one asked should be doubled to the other. The Covetous Man, that thought he could never have enough, was a good while at a stand: considering, that let him ask never so much, the other should have twice as much; but he came however by degrees, to pitch upon one thing after another, and his companion had it double. It was now the Envious Man's turn to offer up his request, which was, that one of his own eyes might be put out, for his companion was then to lose both.

112

A Crow and a Pitcher

A CROW THAT was extreme thirsty, found a Pitcher with a little water in't, but it lay so low he could not come at it. He tried first to break the pot, and then to overturn it, but it was both too strong, and too heavy for him. He bethought himself however of a device at last that did his business; which was, by dropping a great many little pebbles into the water, and raising it that way, till he had it within reach.

113

A Man and a Satyr

THERE WAS A Man and a Satyr that kept much together. The Man clapped his fingers one day to his mouth, and blew upon 'em. What's that for? (says the Satyr). Why, says he, my hands are extreme cold, and I do't to warm 'em. The Satyr, at another time, found this Man blowing his porridge; and pray, says he, what's the meaning of that now? Oh! says the Man, my porridge are hot, and I do't to cool 'em. Nay, says the Satyr, if you have gotten a trick of blowing hot and cold out of the same mouth, I have e'en done with ye.

114

A Bull and a Mouse

A MOUSE PINCHED a Bull by the foot, and then slunk into her hole. The Bull tears up the ground upon't, and tosses his head in the air, looking about, in a rage, for his enemy, but sees none. As he was in the height of his fury, the Mouse puts out her head, and laughs at him. Your pride (says he) may be brought down I see, for all your blustering, and your horns; for here's a poor Mouse has got the better of ye, and you do not know how to help yourself.

115

A Countryman and Hercules

A CARTER THAT had laid his wagon fast in a slough, stood gaping and bawling to as many of the Gods and Goddesses as he could muster up, and to Hercules especially, to help him out of the mire. Why ye lazy puppy you, says Hercules, lay your shoulder to the wheel, and prick your oxen first, and then's your time to pray. Are the Gods to do your drudgery, d'ye think, and you lie bellowing with your finger in your mouth?

116

A Hen and Golden Eggs

A CERTAIN GOOD woman had a Hen, that laid her Golden Eggs, which could not be, she thought, without a mine in the belly of her. Upon this presumption she cut her up to search for hidden treasure; but upon the dissection found her just like other Hens, and that the hope of getting more had betrayed her to the loss of what she had in possession.

117

A Fox and a Hedgehog

ÆSOP BROUGHT THE Samians to their wits again out of a most desperate sedition with this fable

A Fox, upon the crossing of a river, was forced away by the current into an eddy, and there he lay with whole swarms of flies sucking and galling of him. There was a water Hedgehog (we must imagine) at hand, that in pure pity offered to beat away the flies from him. No, no, says the Fox, pray let 'em alone, for the flies that are upon me now are e'en bursting-full already, and can do me little more hurt than they have done; but when these are gone once, there will be a company you shall see of starved hungry wretches to take their places, that will not leave so much as one drop of blood in the whole body of me.

118

A Husbandman and Ceres

A CERTAIN FARMER complained that the beards of his corn cut the reapers' and the threshers' fingers sometimes, and therefore he desired Ceres that his corn might grow hereafter without beards. The request was granted, and the little birds ate up all his grain. Fool that I was (says he), rather to lose the support of my life, than venture the pricking of my servants' fingers.

119

A Countryman and an Ass

AS A COUNTRYMAN was grazing his Ass in a meadow, comes a hot alarm that the enemy was just falling into their quarters. The poor man calls presently to his Ass, in a terrible fright, to scour away as fast as he could scamper; for, says he, we shall be taken else. Well, quoth the Ass, and what if we should be taken? I have one pack-saddle upon my back already, will they clap another a top of that d'ye think? I can but be a slave wherever I am; so that taken, or not taken, 'tis all a case to me.

120

The Fishes and the Frying Pan

A COOK WAS frying a dish of live Fish, and so soon as ever they felt the heat of the pan: There's no enduring of this, cried one, and so they all leapt into the fire; and instead of mending the matter, they were worse now than before.

121

A Rich Man and a Foolish Servant

A RICH MAN had a certain block-headed fellow to his Servant, and the master would be saying to him at every turn: Well! thou art the very prince of fools! I would I were, says the Man, in a saucy huff once, for I should be the greatest Emperor upon the face of the earth then, and you yourself should be one of my subjects.

122

Town-Dogs and Country-Dogs

'TIS A COMMON thing upon the passing of a strange Dog through a town, to have a hundred curs bawling at his breech, and every yap gets a snap at him. There was one particular Dog, that when he saw there was no saving his skin by running away, turned upon his pursuers, and then found upon the trial, that one set of teeth was worth two pairs of heels; for upon that resolution, they all fell off, and sneaked their way.

123

The Mice and the Oak

THE MICE FOUND it so troublesome to be still climbing the Oak for every bit they put in their bellies, that they were once about to set their teeth to't, and bring the acorns down to them; but some were wiser than some, and a grave experienced Mouse, bade them have a care what they did; for if we destroy our nurse at present, who shall feed us hereafter?

124

A Bear and Bees

A BEAR WAS so enraged once at the stinging of a Bee, that he ran like mad into the bee-garden, and overturned all the hives, in revenge. This outrage brought them out in whole troops upon him; and he came afterwards to bethink himself, how much more advisable it had been to pass over one injury, than by an unprofitable passion to provoke a thousand.

125

A Droll and a Bishop

THERE WAS A roguy wag of a Droll that had a mind once to put a trick upon a hard, close-fisted Bishop; so he went to him upon the First of January to wish him a Merry New Year on't, and begged a Five Guinea piece of him for a New Year's gift. Why, the man's mad (says the Prelate), and I believe he takes me to be so too. Dost think I have so little wit, as to part with such a gob of money for God-a-Mercy? Nay, my Lord (says the fellow), if that be too much, let it be but a single George, and I'll be thankful for't. But that would not do either. He fell next bout to a copper farthing, and was denied that too. When the fellow saw that there was no money to be got: Pray, my Lord (says he), let me beg your blessing then. With all my heart (says the Bishop), down on your knees, and you shall have it. No, my Lord (says t'other), 'tis my turn now to deny; for if you yourself had thought that blessing worth a copper farthing, you'd never have parted with it.

126

A Huntsman and a Currier

A CURRIER BOUGHT a bear-skin of a Huntsman, and laid him down ready money for't. The Huntsman told him that he would kill a bear next day, and he should have the skin. The Currier, for his curiosity, went out with the Huntsman to the chase, and mounted a tree, where he might see the sport. The Huntsman advanced very bravely up to the den where the bear lay, and threw in his dogs upon him. He rustled out immediately, and the man missing his aim, the bear overturned him. So the fellow held his breath, and lay stone still, as if he were dead. The bear snuffled, and smelt to him; took him for a carcass, and so left him. When the bear was gone, and the danger over, down comes the Currier from the tree, and bade the Huntsman rise. Hark ye, my friend, says the Currier, the bear whispered somewhat in your ear, what was it, I prithee? Oh (says the Huntsman), he bade me have a care for the future to make sure of the bear before I sell his skin.

127

A Counsel of Birds for choosing more Kings

THE BIRDS WERE mightily possessed with an opinion, that it was utterly impossible for the eagle alone to administer equal justice to all her subjects; and upon this ground, there was a motion put up, for changing the monarchy into a republic; but an old cunning crow, that saw further into a millstone than his neighbours, with one word of his mouth dashed the project. The more kings you have, says he, the more sacks there are to be filled. And so the debate fell.

128

A Cat and Mice

AS A COMPANY of Mice were peeping out of their holes for discovery, they spied a Cat upon a shelf, that lay and looked so demurely, as if there had been neither life nor soul in her. Well (says one of the Mice) that's a good natured creature, I'll warrant her; one may read it in her very looks; and truly I have the greatest mind in the world to make an acquaintance with her. So said, and so done; but so soon as ever Puss had her within reach, she gave her to understand, that the face is not always the index of the mind.

129

A Hedgehog and a Snake

A SNAKE WAS prevailed upon in a cold winter, to take a Hedgehog into his cell; but when he was once in, the place was so narrow, that the prickles of the Hedgehog were very troublesome to his companion: so that the Snake told him, he must needs provide for himself somewhere else, for the hole was not big enough to hold them both. Why then, says the Hedgehog, he that cannot stay shall do well to go; but for my own part, I am e'en content where I am, and if you be not so too, y'are free to remove.

130

An Impertinent and a Philosopher

A CERTAIN PRAGMATICAL, senseless companion would make a visit to a Philosopher. He found him alone in his study, and fell a wondering how he could endure to lead so solitary a life; the learned man told him: Sir, says he, you are exceedingly mistaken; for I was in very good company till you came in.

131

A Sheep-biter Hanged

A CERTAIN SHEPHERD had one favourite dog, that he had a particular confidence in above all the rest. He fed him with his own hand, and took more care of him, in short, than of any of his fellows. This kindness went on a long time, 'till in conclusion, upon the missing of some sheep, he fancied this cur to be false to him; after this jealousy, he kept a strict eye upon him, and in fine, found it out, that this trusty servant of his was the felon. Upon the discovery, he had him presently taken up, and bade him prepare for execution. Alas! master, says the dog, I am one of your family, and 'twould be hard to put a domestic to extremities; turn your displeasure upon the wolves rather, that make a daily practice on't to worry your sheep. No, no, says the shepherd, I'd sooner spare forty wolves that make it their profession to kill sheep, than one sheep-biting cur that's trusted with the care of them. There's somewhat of frankness and generosity in the one; but the other is the basest of treacheries.

132

Industry and Sloth

ONE WAS ASKING a lazy young fellow what made him lie in bed so long? Why (says he), I am hearing of causes every morning; that is to say, I have two pleaders at my bedside so soon as ever I wake. Their names are Industry and Sloth; one bids me get up; t'other bids me lie still; and so they give me twenty reasons why I should rise, and why I should not. 'Tis the part in the meantime of a just judge to hear what can be said on both sides; and before the cause is over, 'tis time to go to dinner.

133

A Cock and a Fox

A FOX SPIED a Cock at roost with his hens about him. Why how now my friend, says Reynard, what make you upon a tree there? Your business lies upon the terra firma, and a Cock in the air is out of his element methinks. But you don't hear the news perhaps, and it is certainly true: there's a general peace concluded among all living creatures, and not one of them to presume upon pain of life and limb, directly or indirectly, to hurt another. The blessedest tidings in the world, says the Cock; and at the same time he stretches out his neck, as if he were looking at somewhat a great way off. What are you peering at? says the Fox. Nothing says t'other, but a couple of great dogs yonder that are coming this way, open mouth, as hard as they can drive. Why then, says Reynard, I fancy I'd e'en best be jogging. No, no, says the Cock, the general peace will secure you. Ay, quoth the Fox, so it will; but if these roguy curs should not have heard of the proclamation, my coat may come to be pinked yet for all that. And so away he scampered.

134

A Woman Drowned

AN UNFORTUNATE WOMAN happened to be drowned, and her poor husband was mightily in pain to find out the body; so away he goes along the bank up the course of the river, asking all he met still, if they could tell him any tidings of the body of his dear wife, that was overturned in a boat at such a place below. Why, if you'd find your wife, they cried, you must look for her down the stream. No, no, says the man, my wife's will carried her against wind and tide all the days of her life; and now she's dead, which way soever the current runs, she'll be sure to be against it.

135

An Old Man and an Ass

AN OLD MAN and a little boy were driving an Ass before them to the next market to sell. Why have you no more wit (says one to the Man upon the way), than you and your son to trudge it afoot, and let the Ass go light. So the Man set the boy upon the Ass, and footed it himself. Why Sirrah, says another after this to the boy, ye lazy rogue you, must you ride, and let your ancient father go afoot? The Man, upon this, took down his boy, and got up himself. D'ye see (says a third) how the lazy old knave rides himself, and the poor little child has much ado to creep after him! The father, upon this, took up his son behind him. The next they met, asked the Old Man whether his Ass were his own or no? He said Yes. Troth, there's little sign on't says t'other, by your loading him thus. Well, says the fellow to himself, and what am I to do now? For I am laughed at, if either the Ass be empty, or if one of us rides, or both. And so in the conclusion he bound the Ass's legs together with a cord, and they tried to carry him to market with a pole upon their shoulders betwixt them. This was sport to everybody that saw it, insomuch that the old fellow in great wrath threw down the Ass into a river, and so went his way home again. The good man, in fine, was willing to please everybody, but had the ill fortune to please nobody, and lost his Ass into the bargain.

136

A Country Fellow and a Hog

IN A CERTAIN country, where it was the custom for any man that killed a Hog, to invite the neighbourhood to supper with him, a curmudgeonly fellow that had a Hog to kill, advised with one of his companions how he might save the charge of that supper. Why (says he) do but give it out tomorrow morning, that the Hog was stolen the night before; set a good face on't, and your work is done. Away goes this man open-mouth, next morning, bawling it about, that his Hog was stolen. Right, right, says his comrade, roar it out as I bade you. Ay, but says the Hog-merchant, with damned oaths and imprecations, my Hog is stolen in good earnest. Upon my life, says t'other, thou dost it rarely. So the one swore on, and the other fooled on, till in the conclusion the churl found he was bantered out of his Hog; for the Hog was stolen indeed.

137

A Physician that cured Madmen

THERE WAS A Physician in Milan that took upon him to cure madmen; and his way was this: they were tied naked to a stake, and then set upright in a nasty puddle, deeper or shallower, according to the degree of the distemper; and there to continue, till betwixt cold and hunger they might be brought to their wits again. There was one among the rest, that after fifteen days' soaking began to shew some signs of amendment; and so got leave of the keeper for the liberty of the court, and the house, upon condition not to set foot over the threshold of the street doors. He passed his promise, and was as good as his word.

As he was standing one day at the outer-gate, there came a falconer riding by, with his kites and his curs, and all his hawking trade about him. Heark ye Sir, says the Madman, a word with you. And so he fell to asking him twenty idle questions, what was this, and what was that, and t'other? And what was all this good for? and the like. The gentleman gave him an answer to everything in form. As for example, This that I ride upon (says he), is a horse, that I keep for my sport; and this bird upon my fist is a hawk that catches my quails and partridges; and those dogs are spaniels to spring my game. That's well, says the fool, and what may all the birds be worth now, that you catch in a twelve-month? Why it may be some ten or fifteen pound perhaps, says t'other. Ay but (says the Mad fellow again), what may all your hawks, dogs, and horses cost you in a year? Some fifteen times as much perchance, says the falconer. Get you out of the way then immediately (cried the fool), before our doctor gets sight of you; for if he soused me up to the middle in the pond, you'll be in as sure as a gun up to the ears if he can but set eye on ye.

138

A Country Fellow climbing a Tree

A COUNTRY FELLOW got an unlucky tumble from a Tree. Why this 'tis (says a passenger), when people will be doing things hand over head, without either fear or wit: now could I have taught you a way to climb a thousand Trees, and never hurt yourself with a fall. Alas, says t'other, the advice comes too late for this bout, but let's have it however; for a body may be the better for't another time. Why then (says the traveller), you must take care for the future, whenever you climb another Tree, that you come no faster down than you went up.

139

A Countryman with his Asses

A COUNTRYMAN THAT had been at market with his corn, and was driving his Asses home again, mounted one of the best of them to ease himself. When he was up, he fell to counting, and so kept telling them over and over, all the way he went, but still wanted one of his number. Upon this, away he goes to the market town, whence he came (a matter of seven miles off) back again, enquiring of all he met, if anybody had seen his Ass. He could learn no tidings of him, and so home he went, late at night, as arrant a fool, as he set out. The loss went to the heart of him, but upon alighting, and his wive's[18] giving him the hint, he found his beast again, and that the Ass he rode upon was forgot in the reckoning.

---

18 Wive's is the possessive case of Wife.

140

A Man that carried his Plough to ease his Oxen

A PEASANT THAT had ploughed himself and his Oxen quite aweary, mounted an ass, with the Plough before him, and sent the Oxen to dinner. The poor ass, he found, was ready to sink under the load, and so he took up the Plough and laid it upon his own shoulders. Now, says he to the Ass, thou mayst carry me well enough, when I carry the Plough.

141

Jupiter's Two Wallets

WHEN JUPITER MADE man, he gave him two satchels; one for his neighbour's faults, t'other for his own. These bags he threw over his shoulders, and the former he carried before him, the other behind. So that this fashion came up a great while ago it seems, and it has continued in the world ever since.

142

A Merchant and a Seaman

A MERCHANT AT sea was asking the ship's master, what death his father died? He told him that his father, his grandfather, and his great grandfather were all drowned. Well, says the Merchant, and are not you yourself afraid of being drowned too? No, not I, says the skipper. But pray, says t'other again, what death did your father, grandfather, and great grandfather die? Why they died all in their beds, says the Merchant. Very good, says the skipper, and why should I be any more afraid of going to sea, than you are of going to bed?

143

Mice, Cat, and a Bell

THERE WAS A devillish sly Cat it seems in a certain house, and the Mice were so plagued with her at every turn, that they called a court to advise upon some way to prevent being surprised. If you'll be ruled by me (says a member of the board), there's nothing like hanging a Bell about the Cat's neck, to give warning beforehand, when Puss is a coming. They all looked upon't as the best contrivance that the case would bear. Well (says another) and now we are agreed upon the Bell, say who shall put it about the Cat's neck. There was nobody in fine that would undertake it, and so the expedient fell to the ground.

144

An Ass and a Lion

IN OLD TIME, when a generous beast made more conscience of his word than many a modern Christian has done of an oath, a Lion shook hands with an Ass, and so they agreed upon't to jog on up and down in the woods, lovingly and peaceably together. As they were upon this adventure, they discovered a herd of wolves; the Ass immediately sets up a hideous bray, and fetches a run at them open mouth, as if he would have eaten 'em. The wolves only sneered at him for his pains, but scampered away however as hard as they could drive. By and by comes the Ass back again, puffing and blowing from the chase. Well, says the Lion, and what was that horrid scream for, I prithee? Why (says t'other) I frightened 'em all away, you see. And did they run away from you, says the Lion, or from me, d'ye think?

145

Boys and Frogs

A COMPANY OF waggish Boys were watching of Frogs at the side of a pond, and still as any of 'em put up their heads, they'd be pelting them down again with stones. Children (says one of the Frogs), you never consider, that though this may be play to you, 'tis death to us.

146

A Council of Beasts

THE BEASTS (A great while ago) were so harassed out with perpetual feuds and factions, that they called a general council, in the nature of a committee of grievances, to advise upon some way for the adjusting of differences, in order to a public peace. After a great many notable things said upon the debate, pro and con, the hares at last (according to the printed votes of those days) delivered their sense to this effect: There can never be any quiet in this world, so long as one Beast shall be allowed nails, teeth, or horns, more than another; but the weaker will still be a prey to the stronger: wherefore we humbly propose a universal parity, and that we may be all upon the same level, both for dignity and power; for we may then, and not till then, promise ourselves a blessed state of agreement, when no one creature shall be able to hurt another.

147

Two Travellers find an Oyster

AS TWO MEN were walking by the sea-side, at a low water, they saw an Oyster, and they both pointed at it together. The one stoops to take it up; the other gives him a push, and tells him, 'tis not yet decided whether it shall be yours or mine. In the interim, while they were disputing their title to't, comes a passenger that way, and to him they referred the matter by consent, which of the two had the better right to the Oyster. The arbitrator very gravely takes out his knife, and opens it; the plaintiff and defendant at the same time gaping at the man, to see what would come on't. He loosens the fish, gulps it down, and so soon as ever the morsel was gone the way of all flesh, wipes his mouth, and pronounces judgment. My masters (says he, with the voice of authority), the court has ordered each of ye a shell, without costs; and so pray go home again, and live peaceably among your neighbours.

148

A Boar Challenges an Ass

THERE PASSED SOME hard words betwixt a Boar and an Ass, and a challenge followed upon't. The Boar depended upon his tusks, and computed within himself, that head to head t'other could never be able to encounter him. So he advanced upon his adversary; and the Ass, so soon as ever he had him within distance, turned tail upon him, and gave him such a lash over the chops with his iron hoof, that he made him stagger again. The Boar after a little pause, recovered himself, Well (says he) I was not aware of such an attack from that end.

149

An Ass and a Shadow

ONE HIRED AN Ass in the dog-days to carry certain
bales of goods to such a town. 'Twas extreme hot,
so that he lay down upon the way to refresh himself
under the shade of the Ass. The muleteer bade him
rise, and go on according to his bargain. T'other
said that the Ass was his for the time he had hired
him. Right, says the other, you have hired the Ass,
but not the Shadow.

150

A Lion and a Man

AMONG OTHER GOOD counsels that an old experienced Lion gave to his whelp, this was one: that he should never contend with a Man; for, says he, if ever you do, you'll be worsted. The little Lion gave his father the hearing, and kept the advice in his thought, but it never went near his heart. When he came to be grown up afterward, and in the flower of his strength and vigour, about and about he ranges to look for a Man to grapple with; in his ramble he chances to spy a yoke of oxen; so up to 'em he goes presently. Hark ye friends, says he, are you men? They told him No; but their master was a Man. Upon leaving the oxen, he went to a horse, that he saw bridled, and tied to a tree, and asked him the same question. No, says the horse, I am no Man myself, but he that bridled and saddled me, and tied me up here, he's a Man. He goes after this to one that was cleaving of blocks. D'ye hear, says the Lion, you seem to be a Man. And a Man I am, says the fellow. That's well, quoth the Lion, and dare you fight with me? Yes, says the Man, I dare fight with ye; why I can tear all these blocks to pieces ye see. Put your feet now into this gap, where you see an iron thing there, and try what you can do. The Lion presently put his claws into the gaping of the wood, and with one lusty pluck, made it give way, and out drops the wedge, the wood immediately closing upon't; and there was the Lion caught by the toes. The woodman presently upon this raises the country; and the Lion finding what a strait he was in, gave one hearty twitch, and got his feet out of the trap, but left his claws behind him. So away he goes back to his father, all lame and bloody, with this confession in his mouth. Alas, my dear father, says he, this had never been if I had followed your advice.

151

A Consultation about securing a Town

THERE WAS A council of mechanics called to advise about the fortifying of a city; a bricklayer was for walling it with stone; a carpenter was of opinion, that timber would be worth forty on't: and after them, up starts a currier: Gentlemen, says he, when y'ave said all that can be said, there's nothing in the world like leather.

152

A Boy that would not learn his Book

THERE WAS A stomachful[19] boy put to school, and the whole world could not bring him to pronounce the first letter of his alphabet. Open your mouth, says the master, and cry *A*. The Boy gapes, without so much as offering at the vowel. When the master could do no good upon him, his school-fellows took him to task among themselves. Why 'tis not so hard a thing methinks, says one of 'em to cry *A*. No, says the Boy, 'tis not so hard neither; but if I should cry *A* once, they'd make me cry *B* too, and I'll never do that, I'm resolved.

---

19 Obstinate.

153

A Rich Man and a Poor

AS A POOR fellow was beating the hoof upon the highway, and trudging on merrily in a bitter cold morning, with never a rag to his tail, a spark that was warm clad, and well mounted (but his teeth chattering in his head yet) called to this tatter-de-mallion, and asked him how he was able to endure this terrible weather? Why, says t'other, how does your face endure it? My face is used to't, says the Cavalier. And so is my body, says the other; so that I am all face.

154

Three Dreaming Travellers

THREE MEN WERE travelling through a wilderness;
the journey it seems was longer than they thought
for, and their provisions fell short; but there was
enough left for anyone of 'em yet, though too little
for all; and how to dispose of the remainder, was
the question. Come (says one of the three) let's e'en
lie down and sleep, and he that has the strangest
dream, shall have that's left. The motion was agreed
to, and so they disposed themselves to their rest.
About midnight, two of them waked, and told one
another their dreams. Lord, says one of 'em, what
a fancy have I had! I was taken up methought into
the Heavens, I know not how, and there set down
just before Jupiter's throne. And I, says t'other,
was hurried away by a whirlwind, methought to
the very pit of hell. The third all this while slept
dog-sleep, and heard every word they said. They
fell then to lugging and pinching their companion,
to tell him the story. Nay, pray be quiet, says he,

what are ye? Why we are your fellow travellers, they cried. Are ye come back again then? says he. They told him they had never stirred from the place where they were. Nay then, says t'other, 'twas but a dream, for I fancied that one of ye was carried away with a whirlwind to Jupiter, and t'other to Pluto; and then thought I to myself, I shall never see these poor people again; so I e'en fell on, and ate up all the victuals.

155

An Ass carrying an Image

AS AN ASS was carrying an Image in procession, the people fell everywhere down upon their knees before him. This silly animal fancied that they worshipped him all this while; till one rounded him in the ear; and told him: Friend, says he, you are the very same Ass with this burden upon your back, that you were before you took it up; and 'tis not the brute they bow to, but the Image.

ALSO FROM CARRIGBOY

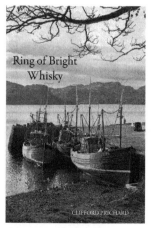

Ring of Bright Whisky

The nostalgic, humorous, poignant – and true – account of the adventures in the Seventies of a successful PR man to an underwear company in the City who, after opting-out of the rat-race to a life of self-sufficiency in the wilds of the Scottish Highlands, finds that all the authors of all the books that have fed his dreams only seem to have told half the story. This book sets out to tell the other half.

ISBN 978-1-910388-05-1

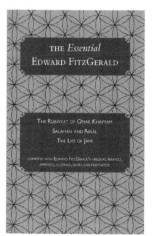

THE *Essential* EDWARD FITZGERALD

Here in one volume are the collected chief works of the Victorian writer and poet, EDWARD FITZGERALD, complete with original notes, prefaces, glossary and appendix.

For the great majority of English readers, the Rubáiyát of Omar Khayyám means only these particular translations, the first, second and fifth editions done so divinely well by FitzGerald, when the Victorian Age of Empire was at its height.

Here also is his less well-known translation of the mystical Súfi allegory, Salámán and Absál, by the Persian scholar and poet, Jámí, as well as FitzGerald's biographies of both Omar Khayyám and Jámí.

ISBN 978-1-910388-02-0

Made in the USA
Middletown, DE
05 March 2017